THE WOMAN OF TEKOAH

THE WOMAN
OF
TEKOAH

And Other Sermons on
Bible Characters

CLARENCE EDWARD MACARTNEY

ABINGDON PRESS
NEW YORK · NASHVILLE

THE WOMAN OF TEKOAH

Copyright MCMLV by Pierce & Washabaugh

Library of Congress Catalog Card Number: 55-5397

SET UP, PRINTED, AND BOUND BY THE
PARTHENON PRESS, AT NASHVILLE,
TENNESSEE, UNITED STATES OF AMERICA

PREFACE

ALMOST AS FAR BACK AS I CAN REMEMBER, BIBLE
biography has intrigued me. At the very start of my ministry I began to write and preach sermons on the characters of the Bible. One of the very first was a sermon on
Esther, whose history affords a splendid background for a
sermon on divine providence. Another was a sermon on
"Sisera and the Lordly Dish."

These two sermons, one a sermon on providence, and
God in history, and the other a sermon on temptation,
are indicative of the wide range of pulpit themes which
Bible biography opens up for the preacher. There is not a
doctrine of the Christian faith, not a duty of the Christian
believer, not a temptation which assails the soul of man,
which cannot be illustrated by some Bible character.

Of necessity, a sermon on one of the personalities of
the Bible has the ring of reality about it, whether it deals
with man's sorrows, his doubts, his temptations, or his
wonder about the life after death; for man's nature is ever
the same, whether he is a man out of the book of Genesis,
out of the New Testament, or out of our own day.

Preaching for half a century now on Bible characters
has been a stirring and inspiring labor for me as a
preacher; not altogether, I hope, without profit to the
congregation; and, it may be, of suggestion to other
preachers.

CLARENCE EDWARD MACARTNEY

CONTENTS

I

II

III

IV

V

VI

I

THE WOMAN OF TEKOAH
How God Brings Home His Own

> "Yet doth he devise means, that
> his banished be not expelled from him."
> II Sam. 14:14

AN OBSCURE AND HUMBLE WOMAN, OF AN OBSCURE
village in Israel, almost three thousand years ago, utters
a single sentence; but that sentence has made the Woman
of Tekoah immortal.

DAVID'S SORROW

Sunset in David's holy and royal city. The south wind,
whose sweet benediction travelers in that land will always remember, has commenced to blow softly. The king
of Israel comes on the roof garden of his palace to take
the air. He is a king, and yet on his face there are lines
of care and sorrow. God has given him rest from his
wars and his enemies—the house of Saul, the Ammonites,
the Philistines, and the Amorites. But the most dangerous Philistines and Ammonites are those of a man's own
breast. David has the recollection of his great sin and
grievous fall; and now in the sins and crimes of his sons
he hears the sad echo of his own transgressions.

The king walks to and fro on the roof, pausing now

and then to gaze into the distance, toward the east. Then he reclines on his couch and takes up his harp; the harp which was his companion when he kept the flocks of Jesse beneath the stars at Bethlehem; the harp whose strains drove the evil spirit away from Saul; the harp that has been his solace in every time of trial and danger. But now, after a few strokes, he lays it aside, for today his harp is tuneless.

He rises again and walks to the balustrade and gazes earnestly and wistfully into the distance; and the direction in which he looks is always the same—never northward, where Hermon lifts his snow-crowned head; never southward, where Bethlehem lies, and Hebron, where he was crowned; never westward, where the great sea rolls; but always eastward, toward the Jordan, toward the mountains of Moab, because over there somewhere is the banished Absalom.

For three years now Absalom has been in exile for the murder of his brother Amnon, who ravished Tamar, full sister to Absalom and half sister to Amnon. Yet the heart of the lonely king yearns for his son. That is why he is always looking eastward, across the Jordan, toward the land of Geshur. In David's breast there is a conflict between David the king, the administrator of justice, and David the father. David the king, the upholder of the law, is saying: "Absalom, you are a murderer. You treacherously slew your own brother. You dipped your hand in the blood of Amnon. You have broken the law of God and the law of man. Absalom, remain in exile. Never see my face again."

But David the father is speaking in a far different manner. What David the father is saying is this: "Absalom, come home. Without thee the feast is tasteless; without thee my harp is tuneless; without thee the palace halls are cheerless; without thee the pomp and circumstance of war is but an empty show. Thou hast slain thy brother; yet with all thy faults I love thee still. Absalom, my son, my son Absalom, come home!"

And thus passed the days, the weeks, the months, the years. For three years the "soul of King David longed to go forth unto Absalom." Joab, the captain of the host, David's counselor and friend, and, until the very end of David's life, faithful to him, perceived that the king's heart was toward Absalom; that he was eating his heart out in grief, and unfitting himself for his kingly duties. Joab was sure there was only one cure for David, and that was to bring Absalom home again. But how could that be done?

A WOMAN'S SAD STORY

As David's captain and counselor, Joab felt it would not do for him openly to advise the king to pass over justice and restore Absalom. He therefore hit upon a stratagem. He remembered that in the village of Tekoah, to the south of Bethlehem, there lived a woman who had a reputation for wisdom, tact, and eloquence. Joab knew too there are some things a woman can do better than a man. This was one of them.

He summoned the woman to Jerusalem, and when she came, he told her to put on the garments of sorrow and affliction. Then he put into her mouth a story. Possibly it was a true story, and the woman's history may have been just as she was told to describe it to David. This is the speech Joab put into the woman's mouth. It is one of the four or five great speeches of the Bible: one of them Judah's eloquent plea to Joseph to let Benjamin go home to Jacob with the other brothers; another, Abigail's plea to David to stay his hand when he was on his way to wipe out Nabal and all his house. But nowhere in the Bible is there, in so short a space, a passage which has in it such beautiful metaphors, such pathos and eloquence.

Garbed in the habiliments of deepest grief, the woman of Tekoah fell down in the presence of the king, crying out, "Help, O king!" There comes a time for all of us when that cry is our only language; a time when human wisdom and strength can do no more, and we must have strength from a higher source. Then we must cry, like this woman, "Help, O King! Help, O God! Lead me to the Rock that is higher than I." Either that cry, or stark despair.

The always kind and sympathetic David, telling the woman to rise, said to her, "What aileth thee?" Then the woman told her story. "I am indeed a widow woman, and mine husband is dead. And thy handmaid had two sons, and they two strove together in the field, and there was none to part them, but the one smote the other, and slew him." Alas, how often that has been true—there was none to part them! Because there was none to part them, brother has smitten brother, and son has smitten parent, and husband has smitten wife, and friend has smitten

12

friend; and nations have been at one another's throats. Blessed, indeed, is the peacemaker. But here there was no peacemaker; none to part them.

"And, behold," continued the woman, "the whole family is risen against thine handmaid, and they said, Deliver him that smote his brother, that we may kill him, for the life of his brother whom he slew. . . . And so they shall quench my coal which is left, and shall not leave to my husband neither name nor remainder upon the earth." "My coal which is left"—what pathos and poetry in that metaphor! Her last coal, which glows with the heart of affection for her bereaved soul; her last coal, which glows with the light of hope for her lonely heart.

A moving tale. If the reading of it three thousand years after it was spoken stirs us, it is not strange that it moved David when first it fell from the woman's lips. "Go to thine house," the king said, "and I will give charge concerning thee." The inference was that he would grant the woman's request. Yet he had not definitely said so. The woman wanted definite assurance, and pressed the king further for a word which would assure her that the avengers of blood would not slay her son, her "last coal," and also that she herself would not suffer because she refused to deliver up her son to the avengers. This assurance David gave her: "Whosoever saith aught unto thee, bring him to me, and he shall not touch thee any more. . . . As the Lord liveth, there shall not one hair of thy son fall to the earth."

Now, having carried the outer defenses of David's heart, and had him commit himself concerning her own

13

son, she moved against the inner defenses of his heart to move him to be reconciled to Absalom. With incomparable grace and tact and humility, the woman said to the king: "Let thine handmaid, I pray thee, speak one word unto my Lord the king." Wondering, no doubt, what was coming, the king said, "Say on."

HER ELOQUENT PLEA

In effect, this is what she said. "Thou, O king, hast pardoned my son who slew his brother, and thus saved him from the hand of the avengers. But what, O king, of thine own son, who slew his brother? Thou too hast, or hadst, two sons, and Absalom smote Amnon and slew him. True, Amnon's offense was great, and he deserved to die; yet he was treacherously slain by his brother. Now Absalom is banished, and for three long years thou hast not seen his face. If, O king, thou canst pardon the son of thine handmaid, the humblest and the lowest in the realm, then why canst thou not pardon thine own son? Remember, O king, that life is uncertain; at the longest, it is but short; for we must needs die, and are as water spilt on the ground, which cannot be gathered up again." How true that is! If there is any word that ought to be spoken, any reconciliation sought, any ministry of kindness done, wait not until life's precious water has been spilt upon the ground by the hand of death, not to be gathered up again. "Or ever the silver cord be loosed, or the golden bowl be broken, or the pitcher be broken at the fountain, or the wheel broken at the cistern."

"I must die, O king; and thou also, and Absalom too;

and if thou shouldest die first, or Absalom first, then there can be no forgiveness and no reconciliation. Amnon is dead; he shall not return to thee. No severity to Absalom can bring Amnon back. Why, then, O king, wilt thou not pardon Absalom and bring him home? Is not that what God himself does? Are we not all banished from God by our sins? Yet doth not God devise means that his banished be not expelled from him?"

With that moving appeal the woman carried David's heart and persuaded him to do what he himself had been longing to do—bring Absalom home. But David felt certain there was someone other than this woman in this carefully worked-out plan to have him commit himself in such a way, in a supposititious, perhaps real, case, that he could hardly refuse to pardon Absalom. He said to the woman: "Is not the hand of Joab with thee in all this?" The woman said it was so, and confessed that it was Joab who had brought her to the court and put the words in her mouth. Dismissing the woman, David summoned Joab, who was waiting, no doubt, in an antechamber to see what the issue of his stratagem would be. When he came in, the king said: "Behold now, I have done this thing: go therefore, bring the young man Absalom again."

A thousand years before Christ died on the cross, this humble woman of Tekoah, pleading with David to forgive Absalom, banished for his sin, consciously or unconsciously uttered a word that gives her a sure place among the prophets and apostles who have spoken of God's mightiest and sublimest work, the atonement of Christ for man's sin upon the cross. "Yet doth God de-

vise means, that his banished be not expelled from him."
Let us then give our thought to this grand central fact
and truth of our holy faith, and speak of the "glorious
gospel of the blessed God."

MAN BANISHED FROM GOD

In the first place, man is banished from God by sin. Up
to a certain point, there is a similarity and parallel between
the story of David and Absalom and the story of how God
brings back man, the sinner. Absalom's crime had banished him from the face of his father. He no longer had a
right to the king's court. Man's sin has banished him from
the presence of God, and he no longer has a "right to the
tree of life." That is what sin has ever been doing, sepa-
rating man from God. As the old Catechism truly phrased
it, by the Fall man "lost communion with God." That is
not sixteenth-century theology; it is as recent and modern
as the last man or woman who has sinned and immediately
known that a cloud has come between himself and God.
The man and the woman sinned, and hid themselves from
the presence of God; Cain sinned, and went out from the
presence of God; Jacob sinned against his father and
brother, and went out from his home into far-off Mesopo-
tamia; Gehazi sinned, and went out from Elisha's presence
a leper as white as snow; Peter sinned, and went out
from the presence of Jesus, and wept bitterly; Judas sinned,
and went out, and it was night. Always out; always away
from the presence of God. "Your iniquities," said the
prophet, "have separated between you and your God, and
your sins have hid his face from you, that he will not hear."

16

Christianity is not a religion for angels, but a religion for sinners. It is a religion for banished souls. Hence the Scriptures speak of it as the "word of reconciliation" and the "ministry of reconciliation."

LOVE FOR A BANISHED SON

The second parallel between the story of David and Absalom and that of God and his banished sons is that as David still loved Absalom—his "soul longed to go forth unto him"—so God still loves the son whose sin has banished him from his presence. Very moving, indeed, is an earthly parent's love for a son who has gone astray.

It was a mansion of wealth and culture. The hostess was showing me through the house and pointing out the paintings and portraits on the walls. At length we came to the portrait of one whom I at once recognized as her son, a notorious criminal. I wondered what she would say as we paused beneath it. This is all she said—but it was everything—"Poor Harry!"

Yet David's love for Absalom was not strange. Blackguard though Absalom was, he was David's son, part of his body and soul. Moreover, when David loved Absalom, we must remember, it was one sinner loving another. But the marvel of God's love for man is that the holy and sinless God can, and does, love the sinner. When that man and woman who committed the crime of the century, the kidnaping of the Greenlease child, paid for it with their lives in the Missouri gas chamber, was there anyone in the whole land who loved them? Yet God loves the sinner. It is hard for us to love the unworthy and the unlovable.

But that is what God does. "Scarcely for a righteous man will one die: yet peradventure for a good man some would even dare to die. But God commendeth his love toward us, in that, while we were yet sinners, Christ died for us." It was the thought of that which brought the doxologies leaping from the lips of the apostles.

How much God loves us, how greatly his "soul longs to go forth" to his banished sons, and how far God's love drove his mercy, Jesus told us in those three great parables: first, the woman who lost one of her ten pieces of silver, and lighted her candle, and took her broom and swept every corner of her house until she found it. So God with the broom of the Cross sweeps the dark places of the earth to find that which was lost. Then the shepherd who had a hundred sheep; but when one, only one, was missing, left the ninety-and-nine in the fold, and went out into the wilderness, and over the dark mountains, and searched until he found it; and when he had found it, laid it over his shoulder, rejoicing. And last of all that father who lost one of his sons, but whose love followed that lost son far down into the far country until the son repented, and said:

I will arise and go unto my father, and will say unto him, Father I have sinned against heaven, and before thee.
And when he was yet a great way off, his father saw him, . . . and ran, and fell on his neck, and kissed him, . . . and said to his servants, Bring forth the best robe, and put it on him; and put a ring on his hand, and shoes on his feet; . . . for this my son was dead, and is alive again; he was lost, and is found.

BRINGING BACK THE LOST

We come now to how God finds and brings back that which was lost. Here the parallel between God and David breaks down. David sent Joab to bring Absalom home. But Joab could do nothing to change the mind and heart of Absalom and bring him to repentance. He came home unchanged, without repentance or sorrow for his sin. Even David, much as he had longed to see Absalom's face, now refused to see him for two long years. What was the result of that kind of forgiveness and reconciliation? The result was that Absalom "stole the hearts" of the people and conspired against his father, defiled his palace, drove him from his throne, and sought to slay him; the result was the wood of Ephraim strewn with twenty thousand corpses; the result was the once flawless and perfect body of Absalom, now all hacked and mutilated, cast into the pit in the wood like a dead dog, instead of lying yonder in the costly tomb he had built for himself, and covered with the stones and execrations of the soldiers as they marched off the field of battle; the result was David, when he said to the second runner, "Is the young man Absalom safe?" and got the answer, "The enemies of my lord the king, and all that rise up against thee to do thee hurt, be as that young man is," going up the stone stairs to the chamber over the gate, and as he went, thus lamenting: "O my son Absalom, my son, my son Absalom! would God I had died for thee, O Absalom, my son, my son!"

Far different was God's plan of forgiveness and restoration. David sent Joab to bring Absalom home; but God sent his only begotten Son to bring us home. "Yet doth he devise means, that his banished be not expelled from him."

And how great those means! Sometimes you hear men speak of the "simple" gospel. It is indeed simple and unmistakable in its demonstration of God's love; simple in its declaration of man's sin; simple in the ground of our forgiveness, our faith in Christ; but not simple in the means which God devised and employed. No; the very angels, we are told, desire to look into that! How ought God to deal with sin? Could he ignore sin? No; for he is of purer eyes than to behold iniquity. Could he destroy the fallen race? He could have done that with justice; but God is more than justice; God is also love. Could he offer man a cheap forgiveness, a half-way forgiveness, like that which Absalom received? No; that would be unworthy of God.

How to restore man, and yet not overlook his sin; how to remain just and justify man; how to give sin its due and yet pardon the sinner—these were God's problems, and he solved them like a God; solved them in the majesty and mystery of the Cross, where, when the sun hid his face and shut his glories in, when the earth reeled, and the graves of the dead were opened, and the great crimson veil of the temple was rent in twain, Christ was wounded for our transgressions, and bruised for our iniquities, and made intercession for the transgressor. That was God's great plan; that was the mystery hid from the beginning of the world; that was God's secret, which eye had not seen, nor ear heard, neither had entered into the mind of man.

I saw the King upon his throne, and about him stood all the holy angels. From the throne came the word: "Who will go down and redeem my lost creation?" First came forward Uriel, the angel of light, who said: "Father, I will go down. I will show man the light of a perfect example, and, beholding, he will follow the light, and so come back to God." But the Father said: "Beautiful is thy light, Uriel; but now man loves darkness rather than light. Thou art mighty, Uriel, to shine, mighty to illuminate, but thou art not mighty to save."

Then spake Raphael, the angel of the mind: "Father, I will go down, and I will reason with man. I will say, Come, now, let us reason together. By the use of his reason, his mind, man will come back to God." But the Father said: "In vain, Raphael, wilt thou reason with man, for man's mind, man's understanding, has been darkened. Thou art mighty, Raphael, to reason, but thou art not mighty to save."

Then came forward Michael, the angel of the sword, his great two-edged sword flashing and turning in every direction, who said: "Father, I will go down. I will flash before man's eyes my terrible swift sword. I will roll over the world the thunders of thy law, and man will tremble and repent. But the Father said: "In vain, Michael, will be the flashings of thy sword, for man's heart is hardened, and he will not repent. Thou art mighty, Michael, to smite, but thou art not mighty to save."

Then came forward Gabriel, the angel of holy song, who said: "Father I will go down. I will flood the earth with the songs of the angels, with the melody of heaven; and hearing that music, man will turn and come back to God." But the Father said: "In vain, Gabriel, will be the sweet music of thy song, for the ears of fallen man are now stopped, and he will not hear. Thou art mighty to sing, Gabriel, but thou art not mighty to save."

Then came forward the Son himself, he who bore the Second Name in heaven; and before him all the angels and archangels covered their faces, crying, "Holy! Holy! Holy!" Standing before the throne, the Son said: "Father, I will go down. I will divest myself of the glory which I had with thee before the foundation of the world. I will humble myself and take upon me the form of a servant, and become obedient unto death, even the death of the cross. I will be rejected of men, spat upon, crowned with thorns, pierced with nails, and with the lance; and so I shall die; but dying, I shall redeem mankind, for by my death man shall live."

This time I never heard what the Father upon the throne said, for all Heaven rang with the shouts of the angels and archangels, seraphim and cherubim, "Eternal Son, go down! Go down! For thou alone art worthy to die for man. Glory to God in the highest, and on earth, peace, good will to man!"

When David was persuaded to recall Absalom, he said to Joab, "Behold now, I have done this thing: go therefore, bring the young man Absalom again." But it was not *done,* not even half done, for Absalom did not see his father's face. But when Christ cried out amid the gathering darkness of Calvary, "It is finished," it was *done,* completely, gloriously done! When David heard of the death of Absalom in battle, he cried out in his great anguish, "O my son Absalom, my son, my son Absalom! would God I had died for thee!" David, with all his love for him, could not die for Absalom. But Christ died for man, for you and for me. He, and he alone, could do that. "Yet doth God devise means, that his banished be not expelled from him."

Now the banished can come home. The reconciliation has been made; the bridge over the gulf of man's sin has been built; the road is ready; the banners of welcome are hung out. God's banished can come home! There is the gospel; not a part of the gospel, not the important part of the gospel, not the most beautiful part of the gospel, but *the* gospel; and without it there is no gospel. The sinner can come home! God waits to receive you. Have you come? Will you come?

NABOTH

Not for Sale

"And Naboth said to Ahab, The Lord
forbid it me, that I should give the
inheritance of my fathers unto thee."
I Kings 21:3

NABOTH'S REFUSAL WAS THE INTRODUCTION TO ONE OF
the strangest, most powerful, and most terrible dramas of
the Bible; a drama, on one side, of innocence, courage, in-
dependence, and the fear of God, and, on the other side, of
covetousness, avarice, cruelty, perjury, death, and terrible
retribution. Outside of the Bible itself, it would take a
Shakespeare or one of the Greek tragic poets to do justice
to it.

Ahab is one of the best known characters in the Old
Testament. He takes more pages in the Old Testament
than any other worker of iniquity. He stands out all the
more clearly because we see him in contrast with his ad-
versary, the fearless prophet of God, Elijah. Ahab had,
indeed, some residuum of character and the fear of God in
him; but he was under the influence of a Phoenician
tigress, his heathen wife, Jezebel, the murderer of the
prophets. In spite of Ahab's transgressions God had raised
him to great power and had given him victory twice over

the invading armies of the Syrians, led by that inveterate enemy of Israel, Ben-hadad.

Ahab's political capital was at Samaria, high up on the mountaintop, on the road to Jerusalem. But he had built for himself another resort, a sort of *Sans Souci*, at Jezreel, where he lived in an ivory palace, surrounded by all the pleasures and luxuries of royalty. One bright autumn day he was taking a drive in his chariot. As the chariot rolled along the highway, Ahab marked a well-kept vineyard not far from the road. There was a neat hedge about it, a tower, a winepress, and the ground was carefully cultivated. The autumn grapes were purple in the early-afternoon sunlight. Ahab asked his driver to stop so that he could have a look at this vineyard. The more he looked it over, the more he desired to have it. He was the lord, and, in a sense, the owner, of a whole kingdom. He had palaces, soldiers, storehouses, treasures of gold and silver, servants and horses and chariots. Yet he coveted this one small vineyard and was determined to have it. The old myth told of Briareus, who had a hundred arms, a hundred hands. The covetous man is like that. If he had a hundred hands with which to take, that would not be enough. The more he has, the more he wants. The more he gets, the less satisfied he is.

When he got back to his palace at Jezreel, Ahab made inquiry of his courtier, asking him who the owner of this vineyard was. He was told that the owner was a man called Naboth. "Tell him to come to the palace," said Ahab. "I want to talk with him."

25

NABOTH'S REPLY

The messenger found Naboth at his humble home by the vineyard. Wondering what the king could want of him, and perhaps a little disturbed because of what he knew about the king's character, he appeared at the palace. Ahab told him that he wanted his vineyard. He made what would seem to be a fair proposition to Naboth, telling him he would give him in exchange for it a much better vineyard; or, if that did not suit him, he would pay him a large sum of money. To the king's surprise, Naboth said he would not sell the vineyard. "The Lord forbid it me, that I should give thee the inheritance of my fathers unto thee."

There were two reasons why Naboth would not sell. One was that this had always been his home. For generations the vineyard had been in his family. He himself had played there when a boy and toiled there as a man. When life was over for him this vineyard would descend to his sons. He had that fine feeling of attachment to the land which is one of man's best instincts. The other reason why he would not sell was that the law of Moses forbade a man to sell his property and inheritance, except in cases of dire necessity, and then at the year of jubilee it must revert to the owner. This was on the principle that the land belonged to God. Not all Jews were as scrupulous in the matter as Naboth was; but he was a God-fearing man, and felt that it would be an irreligious act, a sin against God, for him to sell his vineyard, even to the king. That was why he said to the king, "The Lord forbid it me, that I should give the inheritance of my fathers unto thee."

The refusal of Naboth to sell greatly displeased and

upset Ahab. By himself he probably would not have thought of stealing or confiscating the vineyard, still less of murdering Naboth to get possession of it. He had ownership of a large part of the land of Israel; and yet, because he could not buy this small piece of property, he was completely out of sorts, displeased, and upset. When the time came for the midday repast in the palace, he would not eat, but, like a spoiled child, flung himself down on his bed and turned his face to the wall.

A WICKED WOMAN

He was in this state of mind when his queen, Jezebel, came into his chamber and asked him what the trouble was. "Why is thy spirit so sad, that thou eatest no bread?" Ahab then told her what had happened—that he had seen a fine vineyard on his drive through the country, and that he had offered the owner of it a much better vineyard in exchange, or, if he preferred, a large sum of money. But the owner would not trade it and would not sell it. The scornful Jezebel said to the king, "Dost thou not govern the kingdom of Israel? Wilt thou permit the owner of a small vineyard to stand in thy way and disregard thy desire? Remember, thou art the king! Arise, and eat bread, and let thine heart be merry: I will give thee the vineyard of Naboth the Jezreelite."

The resolution of the wicked queen, stirring her husband up to a crime that of himself he was afraid to perpetrate, brings to mind the history of Haman. When Haman told his wife, Zeresh, that Mordecai the Jew refused to bow to him, and that all his own honors and high office counted for nothing as long as he saw this Jew refusing to honor him, his wife said, "I will tell you what to do. Build a gallows fifty cubits high, and get the consent of the king to hang Mordecai on it. Then you can go with the king to the banquet, and all will be well." Thus Haman's wife stirred him up to slay a righteous man; only in this case the righteous man escaped, and it was Haman who was hanged.

The plot of Jezebel recalls another cruel, courageous, resourceful, and wicked queen. When Macbeth was frightened as he came to murder the king, Duncan, Lady Macbeth said:

> Infirm of purpose!
> Give me the daggers. The sleeping and the dead
> Are but as pictures; 'tis the eye of childhood
> That fears a painted devil.

THE MURDER OF NABOTH

What Ahab could not devise or do, his fierce consort now craftily executed. She wrote letters in the name of the king to the elders and nobles of the city and sealed them with the royal seal. In the letters she commanded the elders and nobles to proclaim a fast, gather the people together, set Naboth on high in the seat of those who were accused of crime, and then have two sons of Belial testify against him that he had blasphemed God and the king. The elders were then to find Naboth guilty and sentence him to be stoned to death.

This was unsurpassed hypocrisy and cruelty. This Phoenician idolatress, Jezebel, had no regard for God or for the religion of Israel; yet she was going to commit this crime under the guise of religion, having a fast day called for the purpose, and Naboth accused of blaspheming God and of treason and sedition against the king. The elders and nobles knew that this was an outrage and a sin, especially for those who were appointed to be judges in Israel; but they feared Jezebel and did as the letters ordered them to do. The fast was proclaimed; the people assembled, and Naboth was arraigned before the court. Two men rose up, both of them no doubt being paid for it, and said they had heard Naboth speak blasphemy against God and utter treasonable sentiments against the king. Naboth was given no opportunity to answer the charge, but was promptly adjudged guilty and sentenced to death.

I wonder what his feelings and thoughts were before they stoned him to death. Did he say to himself, "Was it a mistake for me to refuse to sell the land? Now I am going to be stoned to death. But if I had sold, I might have had another vineyard, and lived for years in peace. I have feared God and obeyed his law; but now he permits me to be stoned to death." What was in the mind of Naboth we do not know, but we can believe that the man who had the courage on religious grounds to refuse to sell the inheritance of his fathers to the king was not without that mysterious consolation which God gives to those who obey God rather than man.

According to the custom, the witnesses cast the first

stone. Then all the people joined in. Soon all that was left of Naboth was a bloody pulp, the semblance of a man in the image of God all gone. The cowardly elders and nobles who had carried out the terrible orders of Jezebel, the perjured witnesses, and the fickle multitude dispersed and went back to their homes. Naboth, or what remained of him, was left absolutely alone. No, not altogether alone; for the dogs, the scavengers of the East, remained behind and licked up the blood of Naboth.

NABOTH'S CHARACTER

In this terrible tragedy of cruelty, hypocrisy, falsehood, covetousness, murder, injustice, and the death of the righteous, the character of Naboth stands out in magnificent proportions and unforgettable colors. Here was a man upon whose brow was written, "Not For Sale." Naboth was not flattered by the interview with the king, by the invitation to the royal palace. Principle with him meant more than worldly honor. Nor was he influenced by money. He could have asked any price for that vineyard, and the covetous Ahab would have paid it. He could have taken that money and been "well fixed" for life. But there were things which in Ahab's mind counted for more than money. Cynics have said that every man has his price. Even Balaam, in the end, had his price. But not this man; not Naboth. Ahab, as we shall see, and Jezebel, too, had to pay in the end a terrible price for that vineyard. But the high price that Naboth could have asked for it had no influence whatever upon his courageous refusal.

Again, Naboth was not intimidated by the king and his

court. A royal request amounted to a royal command. Naboth well knew that to refuse was dangerous. Yet he stood his ground and died a martyr to conscience. When he heard the terrible charge against him, that he had blasphemed the name of God and that he was guilty of treason against the king, Naboth was unmoved, but stood quietly in the majesty of obedience to conscience, waiting for the first stone.

Naboth is the kind of man that the world needs today. The nation needs that kind of a man. The church needs that kind of a man. Business needs that kind of a man, a man who forgot himself into immortality.

The friends of freedom thought that when Daniel Webster in 1852 delivered his famous Seventh of March Speech, in which he attacked the Abolitionists and, indirectly, defended slavery, he was compromising his principles with the hope that he might gain the presidency. In 1831 Emerson wrote of him these lines:

> Let Webster's lofty face
> Ever on thousands shine;
> A beacon set that freedom's race
> Might gather omens from that radiant sign.

But in 1854 this is what Emerson wrote:

> Why did all manly gifts in Webster fail?
> He wrote on Nature's grandest brow, For Sale.

Governor Adlai Stevenson during the 1952 presidential campaign spoke at the dedication of a monument, at Alton, Illinois. The monument was erected on the spot where on

November 7, 1837, the Presbyterian minister and anti-slavery editor, Elijah Lovejoy, was shot to death trying to protect his printing press from a mob. Governor Stevenson quoted the words which Lovejoy spoke to the mob before he was shot, and splendid words they are, spoken in honor of conscience and in the fear of God: "I am impelled in the course I have taken because I fear God. As I shall answer to God in the great day, I dare not abandon my sentiments nor cease in all proper ways to propagate them. I can die at my post; but I cannot desert it." There was another man who, like Naboth, was not for sale.

RETRIBUTION

The story of Naboth and his vineyard is not only a drama of faith in God and magnificent loyalty to conscience and righteousness, but also a drama of swift and terrible retribution. As soon as Naboth had been stoned to death, Jezebel went in to the sullen king and said to him, "Arise, Naboth is dead, the vineyard is yours. Go down and take possession of it." Ahab arose from the bed where he had been sulking ever since Naboth had refused to sell, put on his royal robes, got into his chariot, and drove down to the vineyard, probably staying as far away as possible from that part of it which was stained with the blood of Naboth. He was starting to walk over the vineyard, and beginning to plan what he would do with it, when lo, he saw a familiar face and a familiar form coming into the vineyard from the other side. It was Elijah the prophet! Before Elijah could speak to the guilty king, Ahab cried out, "Hast thou found me, O mine enemy?"

When a man does wrong, he always has an enemy who is seeking for him, who is on his trail and will one day find him. "Be sure your sin will find you out!" Conscience within the breast can be man's best friend, and would be man's best friend, but it is also his most implacable enemy. "Hast thou found me, O mine enemy?"

Elijah said to the king, "I have found thee: because thou hast sold thyself to work evil in the sight of the Lord. Hear now the word of the Lord. In the place where dogs licked the blood of Naboth shall dogs lick thy blood, even thine." And of Jezebel the prophet said to Ahab, "The dogs shall eat Jezebel by the wall at Jezreel."

Mysterious, divine, inescapable, invincible, inexorable retribution now began to do its work. Ahab, frightened at the prediction of Elijah, rent his clothes, put on sackcloth, and "went softly," and humbled himself before God. But his humility and repentance were short-lived. Three years later, in spite of the warning given him by the prophet of the Lord, Micaiah, he went up to battle with Jehoshaphat against the stronghold of Ramothgilead. The king of the Syrian army commanded his soldiers and his captains to fight neither with small nor with great, save only with the king of Israel. Ahab was frightened. He remembered the prediction of Elijah, and he remembered the prophecy of Micaiah, "I saw all Israel scattered upon the hills, as sheep that have not a shepherd." Thinking to escape his doom, he put off his royal robes and went into battle disguised as a private soldier. But there is no disguise which can hide the sinner from his judgment. A certain man drew a bow at a venture and

33

smote the king of Israel between the joints of his harness. This does not mean that the man was just shooting aimlessly and carelessly, but that he did not know that the officer whom he saw in the ranks of the enemy, driving his chariot up and down, was the king of Israel. But God knew! That unknown soldier was the bowman of divine retribution.

That night Ahab died, and was brought back to his capital. Down by the pool of Samaria the driver of the chariot was washing Ahab's blood out of the chariot. As he did so, the dogs, perhaps the same dogs that had licked up the blood of Naboth, came and licked up the blood which flowed out of Ahab's chariot. "Where the dogs licked the blood of Naboth, the dogs shall lick thy blood, even thine!"

And what of Jezebel, the most guilty in this wicked conspiracy and shameful crime? She reigned on for a time in splendor as the queen-mother in Israel. Her son Joram was now on the throne of Israel, and her grandson Ahaziah on the throne of Judah. But if the mills of the gods grind slowly, they grind "exceeding small." "Careless seems the avenger"; but ever, there, "within the shadow, standeth God, keeping watch above his own."

Elisha, the successor of Elijah, sent a young prophet to anoint Jehu king over Israel. When the young prophet had done so, he told Jehu that he was to be the agent of judgment and retribution upon the house of Ahab. With his armed men Jehu started at once for Jezreel in his chariot. The two kings were taking a sunbath on the roof of the palace, when a watchman reported to them that he saw a cloud of dust in the distance and a company of men approaching. Joram sent out a messenger on horseback, who, when he met the chariot of Jehu, said to him, "Is it peace?" "What has thou to do with peace?" said Jehu. "Turn thee behind me." A second messenger asked the same question and received the same answer. Then Joram himself mounted his chariot and drove out to meet Jehu. When he came up with him, he said, "Is it peace, Jehu?" The avenger answered, "What peace, so long as the whoredoms of thy mother Jezebel are so many?" Hearing this, Joram turned his chariot about and fled. But as he fled, Jehu drew a bow, and the arrow smote Joram between his arms and went out at his heart. This happened just at Naboth's vineyard; and Jehu said to his driver, "Throw him into Naboth's vineyard; for I remember the day when you and I rode with Ahab to this vineyard and heard what Elijah said."

Then the chariot of Jehu thundered on to the wall of the palace. Jezebel now knew what was coming. But she painted her face and darkened her eyes with antimony and tired her head; and thus, a queen, though a wicked one, to the end, she looked out the window, and, taunting Jehu, called out to him, "Had Zimri peace, who slew his master?" Zimri had assassinated the king Bashan and reigned in his place for a few days, only to be burned alive in his palace. Looking up to the window, Jehu called out, "Who is on my side? Who?" When several of the eunuchs, terrified, and ready to desert the queen, looked out of the window, Jehu called to them, "Throw her down! Throw her down!" And down they threw her!

She fell just in front of the horses of Jehu's chariot. The hoofs of the horses and the wheels of the chariot ground her body into the dust. Afterward, while he sat with his followers at the table in the palace, Jehu remembered that Jezebel had been a king's wife and a king's daughter, and the mother of a king, and the grandmother of a king, and perhaps, after all, deserved decent burial, and he said to his followers, "Go take this cursed woman and bury her. She is a king's daughter." But when they went to pick up her body, all that they could find was her skull, her feet, and the palms of her hands. The dogs had taken the rest! Elijah's prediction that day he met Ahab in the vineyard of the murdered Naboth had come true. "The dogs shall eat Jezebel by the wall of Jezreel." Mysterious, terrible, divine retribution!

The way of the transgressor is hard. "Be sure your sin will find you out."

III

JEHOSHAPHAT
He Helped the Ungodly

"Shouldest thou help the ungodly?"
II Chr. 19:2

THAT WAS WHAT JEHOSHAPHAT DID. HE "HELPED the ungodly," although he himself was one of the most godly kings that ever sat upon the throne of Judah. History links Jehoshaphat with one of the most wicked kings of Israel, Ahab. The Bible delights in contrasts: Cain and Abel; Jacob and Esau; David and Saul; John and Judas; Paul and Nero. Very striking, too, is the contrast between these two kings, Jehoshaphat the king of Judah, and Ahab the king of Israel. One tried to destroy the worship of the true God in Israel; the other "sought to the Lord God of his father, and walked in his commandments, and not after the doings of Israel." Whatever in the reign of Jehoshaphat was wrong was due to his association with three wicked kings of Israel, Ahab, Jehoram, and Ahaziah.

COMFORTING THE UNGODLY

There had been much war, and that civil war, the worst of all wars, between the kingdom of Israel and the kingdom of Judah. Together with his reformations, destroying the high places and groves of idolatry out of

37

Judah, and building storehouses and fortresses, and organizing a great army, Jehoshaphat went out of the way to make peace with Israel, even going so far as to marry his son to Athaliah, daughter of Ahab and the fierce Jezebel. When Jehoshaphat made a visit of state to Israel, Ahab gave him a great reception and prolonged entertainment. At the time of his visit, the fortress town of Ramoth-gilead, east of the Jordan, had been taken by the Syrian king, Ben-hadad. Ahab wanted to get back this stronghold and invited Jehoshaphat to go up with him to Ramoth-gilead. Jehoshaphat, pleased with his reception at Ahab's court, and disregarding the evil record of Ahab, accepted the invitation. "I am as thou art, and my people as thy people; and we will be with thee in the war."

Before he set out on this expedition, Jehoshaphat asked Ahab to inquire at the word of the Lord. Ahab was certainly the wrong man to ask to inquire of God, the God whose worship he had tried to destroy in Israel. Nevertheless, he gathered together four hundred time-serving prophets and said to them: "Shall we go to Ramoth-gilead to battle?" With one voice they said, "Go up; for God will deliver it into the king's hand." Jehoshaphat was not pleased either with the looks of these prophets or with their immediate and unanimous assent and approval, and said to Ahab, "Is there not here a prophet of the Lord besides, that we might enquire of him?" Ahab answered, "There is yet one man, by whom we may enquire of the Lord: but I hate him; for he never prophesied good unto me, but always evil." Nevertheless, at Jehoshaphat's insistence, Ahab arranged for the four hundred prophets to

38

appear before the two kings, and also the true prophet of the Lord, Micaiah.

First of all, the four hundred prophets of Ahab appeared at the throne room of the king's ivory palace. On the two thrones sat the two kings, resplendent with their crowns upon their heads and their crimson and purple robes. When the king of Israel, Ahab, asked, "Shall I go against Ramoth-gilead to battle, or shall I forbear?" with an immediate shout the four hundred said: "Go up to Ramoth-gilead, and prosper: for the Lord shall deliver it into the hand of the king." Then the lonely Micaiah stood before the two kings. When they asked him to pronounce upon the proposed expedition against Ramoth-gilead, Micaiah said, "I saw all Israel scattered upon the hills, as sheep that have not a shepherd."

This was a prediction of the defeat and overthrow of Israel in the coming battle and of the death of Ahab. In spite of this warning, Ahab followed the advice of the four hundred false prophets and cast the one true prophet into prison. How often, not only in the great affairs of military operations, but also in the affairs of our own lives, we disregard the voice of the true prophet, the voice of conscience, and follow the clamorous voice of worldly desire or passion! Jehoshaphat must have known that the expedition against Ramoth-gilead would end in disaster, but because he had already given his consent, he joined with Ahab and set out for the fortress town across the Jordan.

Just before the battle was joined with the Syrian army, Ahab became uneasy and frightened. He took off his royal robes and disguised himself, and drove his chariot into the battle as if he were only a subordinate officer in the army. But this ruse could not ward off the arrow of divine retribution. Ahab was slain, and his army scattered, as Micaiah had said, like sheep without a shepherd.

Although the king of Syria, Ben-hadad, had given the command "Fight only with the king of Israel," Jehoshaphat's royal robes drew the attention of the enemy, and it was only by the goodness of God that he escaped the fate of Ahab. When he returned to Jerusalem, one of the prophets met him with this message, a message which must have greatly troubled the good king Jehoshaphat: "Shouldest thou help the ungodly, and love them that hate the Lord? therefore is wrath upon thee from before the Lord."

This godly king, who knew what was right, must have felt deep contrition and humiliation under the judgment of the prophet. By going out to battle with Ahab he had helped the ungodly and created the impression that he loved them that hated the Lord. This is something every Christian man must be on his guard against. It is not enough that one should keep oneself free of open iniquities and transgressions; his daily life should be a reproach, and not an encouragement, to the ungodly. In the book of Ezekiel the prophet pronounced judgment upon Jerusalem because, in spite of God's goodness, the city had become apostate and had done great evil, and thus was a comfort unto Sodom and unto the wicked city of Samaria. What is meant is that these two wicked cities, Sodom and Samaria, had been encouraged in their evil doings by the example of

Jerusalem. "There is Jerusalem," they could say, "the Holy City, the chosen of God. See what her citizens do. If they behave in that way, then surely we need not worry about our conduct."

Comfort for Sodom! A very arresting thought. It brings before us the responsibility of every Christian man, and how he will be held accountable for the influence which he exerts. The life of a good man is a rebuke to evil men and an encouragement and comfort to all who endeavor to do well. Jehoshaphat certainly was not a bad man; yet he permitted himself association with a wicked man and a wicked kingdom.

The church member who neglects the house of worship and prayer is a comfort and encouragement to those who never go. If a Christian man's speech is just as worldly and profane as the speech of a man of the world, then he is a comfort to worldly men. If a woman who is a Christian is just as much of a busybody and gossip and talebearer as the unbelieving woman who lives next to her, she is a comfort and an encouragement to those who do evil. If a Christian man in his business dealings is harder and sharper than an unbeliever, or if he deviates from the course of honor and rectitude and honesty, he is a comfort to all who deal dishonestly and unfairly. If a Christian man laughs just as heartily as a worldly man at a salacious or irreverent anecdote, he comforts all who talk that way. If a Christian man is silent when Christ and his cause and his Church are evil spoken of, his silence encourages all those who are against Christ and his Church.

41

If a Christian man delights to hear and take up an evil report against his neighbor, then he helps the ungodly and is a helper of the calumniator and the slanderer. If a Christian man when he is wronged is just as bitter and harsh and unforgiving as the non-Christian man, then he is an encouragement to all who despise the spirit of Jesus. In one of his passages where he rebukes members of the church at Corinth for bitter and unbrotherly conduct, Paul says, "Are ye not worldly?" That is, "Are ye not behaving just as the unbelievers, the pagans, do?" That is the point. The Christian man confesses to a higher standing. He has committed himself to a different way of life than the world, and for him to depart from that way is not only a sin for him personally, but it also encourages other men to do evil.

MINSTRELS FOR THE SOUL

Before long we hear of this good king Jehoshaphat foolishly joining in another military expedition, not with Ahab this time, but with his wicked son Jehoram. When the king of Moab rebelled against the king of Israel, Jehoram asked Jehoshaphat to go with him to punish Moab. At the end of seven days' march in the barren, arid country to the southeast, the allied armies were like to perish for lack of water. All that the king of Israel could do was to cry out, "Alas! that the Lord hath called these three kings together, to deliver them into the hand of Moab!" But Jehoshaphat said to him, "Is there not here a prophet of the Lord, that we may enquire of the Lord by him?" Jehoram, like his father, was the last man to ask about a prophet of the Lord. But one of the king's servants answered for him, and said that Elisha, who "poured water on the hands of Elijah," was with the army. When Jehoram asked the prophet what they should do, Elisha, in great anger, said to the king of Israel, "What have I to do with thee? get thee to the prophets of thy father, and to the prophets of thy mother. ... As the Lord of hosts liveth, before whom I stand, surely, were it not that I regard the presence of Jehoshaphat the king of Judah, I would not look toward thee, nor see thee!" Nevertheless, for the sake of the good king of Judah, Elisha was willing to exercise his prophetic gift and intercede with God in behalf of the two armies. But he realized that in his angry mood he was in no condition to prophesy. Therefore, he said, "Bring me a minstrel." A wandering minstrel who was with the army was brought before Elisha. As the minstrel touched the strings of his harp, and the soft notes of his music began to float over the desert and the tents of war, the anger in the heart of Elisha began to subside. Now his spirit was calm and tranquil; now he could speak with God, and God could speak with him. "And it came to pass, when the minstrel played, that the hand of the Lord came upon him." Elisha then gave the two kings the directions which delivered them out of their great danger.

There are times in life when we all need the music of the minstrel. When the evil spirit came upon Saul, he would send for David, the shepherd harpist; and as David played upon his harp, perhaps singing, too, one of his psalms, the evil spirit would depart from the unhappy

43

king. Alas, how many evil spirits come down upon us, and how often we need the minstrel to expel these evil spirits from our life! It may be when fierce anger against another flames within the soul; it may be when there is complete lassitude and prostration of the spirit, and we can hardly rouse ourselves to act or choose; it may be the time of sorrow and affliction, when waves of adversity sweep over our life; it may be when the heart has been wounded by the actions of those in whom it put its trust; it may be when the hot whisper of temptation is sounding in our ear; it may be the hour of transgression, when life's fair prospect has been clouded with sin. What we need then is a minstrel for the soul, that we may hear again the voice of God.

The divine minstrel may come through the intervention or faithful counsel of a friend. When David with his four hundred men, marching to the town of the churlish Nabal, who had insulted him and his men, determined to wipe out all his house in blood, Nabal's wife, the beautiful and wise Abigail, met him and persuaded him to sheathe his sword. She pled with him to refrain from shedding blood and avenging himself with his own hand, assuring him that if he followed her advice, when he came at length to the throne of Israel, it would be no grief to him that he had shed blood causeless. The angry David, his wild passion of revenge now subsided, blessed Abigail, saying to her, "Blessed be thy advice, and blessed be thou, which hast kept me this day from coming to shed blood, and from avenging myself with mine own hand."

Worship in God's house is another minstrel for the

soul. The seventy-third psalm tells of a man who was troubled and all but overwhelmed by some trial and difficulty which had come upon him. When he searched his mind and heart to find out why this had come upon him, and to understand it, he got no answer. But when he went to the sanctuary, his burden was lifted. "When I thought to know this, it was too painful for me; until I went into the sanctuary of God; then understood I their end."

The Bible is a sweet minstrel for the soul. When all other books are silent, the Bible still speaks. For every mood in life there comes forth out of its pages a minstrel for the soul. How often it has been, that troubled or sorrowing, tempted or tried, cast down or dismayed, we have found the rhetoric of Psalm 107 transmuted into the gold of actual experience for us: "He sent his word, and healed them, and delivered them from their destructions."

With the Bible goes that other great minstrel, the supreme resource and the last refuge of the soul—prayer. "I sought the Lord, and he heard me, and delivered me from all my fears." In the time of trouble, take God at his word. "Call upon me," he says, "and I will deliver thee." When you are angry and out of sorts, try prayer. When you are tempted to betray your soul, try prayer. When the sun has hidden itself, and all the stars have fled, try prayer. When all his waves and billows have gone over you, try prayer. When doubt clouds your vision, try prayer. When fierce temptations assail, try prayer. When the iron gate bars your path, try prayer. When your sins rise up against you to accuse you, try prayer.

45

THE DISAPPOINTMENTS OF LIFE

We have seen how the good king Jehoshaphat on two different occasions got into serious trouble and narrowly escaped with his life, because, for a time, he had become an ally and companion of two wicked kings, first Ahab, and then the son of Ahab, Jehoram. Now, to our surprise, untaught by experience, Jehoshaphat makes another ill-advised alliance and joins himself with Ahaziah, another son of the wicked Ahab. This time it was an expedition to sail for the gold of Ophir. Ophir was a name that inflamed the imagination of the men of that day as El Dorado, Peru, or Mexico inflamed the imagination of the Spaniards of the sixteenth century. At Ezion-geber, on the shore of the Red Sea, King Solomon had built a navy and sent an expedition to far-off Ophir. The expedition returned with a great quantity of gold with which Solomon embellished his capital. Jehoshaphat and Ahaziah planned to repeat the successful voyage of Solomon, and built their ships at this same Ezion-geber. Perhaps both kings were present when the fleet was ready to sail. With the sound of trumpets, a flourish of banners, and the benediction of royalty, the anchors were weighed, the sails set, and with a favoring wind the armada sailed out of Eziongeber into the Red Sea, bound for far-off Ophir. "But the ships went not," for they were broken on the rocks. A storm arose and drove the ships on the treacherous rocks of the Red Sea. When morning dawned, the proud armada lay strewn on the rocks, a tangled mass of timber and cordage, and all those who had sailed on the ship were buried in the deep. That was the end of the expedition for the gold of Ophir. "They went not; for the ships were broken at Ezion-geber." The fate of the expedition had been foretold by the prophet Eliezer, who warned Jehoshaphat that the expedition would meet with disaster because Jehoshaphat had joined himself with Ahaziah.

We are sorry that Jehoshaphat joined himself with this wicked king Ahaziah, but we are not sorry for this record of disappointed hopes and plans. What is recorded here, that the ships went not, for they were broken on the rocks, is the epitaph for many a hope and dream, and many an expedition of the soul. How many ships never reach their port, but are broken on the rocks! Yet God has a rich ministry for the soul in disappointment. Paul must have been greatly disappointed when, on his way to preach at Ephesus, the great city of the province of Asia, the Spirit of Jesus "suffered him not." He must have been disappointed again when he turned northward, hoping to preach in the rich province of Bithynia on the Black Sea. But again the Spirit of God suffered him not. Unless he turned backward, there was now only one way that the Apostle could go. That brought him straight to the northeast and, at length, to Troas, the ancient Troy. Paul lay down to sleep that night in the Jewish quarter of the city, wondering what God had in store for him. But it was that very night that he had his vision and saw the man from Macedonia, saying to him, "Come over and help us." That dream opened a new epoch in the history of mankind. So God disappoints us, only to lead us on to greater things.

Look at the old man Moses, standing yonder on the

top of Pisgah, gazing with earnest, yearning eye on the Promised Land as it lay unfolded before him across the Jordan. Like an inhalation he drew in all its beauty and glory. But the vision was as brief as an inhalation. God said to him, "I have caused thee to see it with thine eyes, but thou shalt not go over thither." So Moses, the servant of the Lord, died there in the land of Moab, and not in the Promised Land, where he had hoped to die, and was buried in the vale of Moab over against Beth-peor. And no man knoweth of his sepulcher unto this day.

> O lonely grave in Moab's land!
>   O dark Beth-peor's hill!
> Speak to these curious hearts of ours,
>   And teach them to be still.
> God hath his mysteries of grace,
>   Ways that we cannot tell,
> He hides them deep, like the hidden sleep
>   Of him He loved so well.[1]

Now the centuries have rolled away, and Jesus and Peter and James and John have gone up to the mountain-top; and lo, Moses with Elijah appears in glory and talks with Jesus about his coming death on the cross for the sins of the world. Moses was disappointed because God would not let him go over Jordan's flood with the host of Israel. But something far better God has in store for him. Now he appears in the Promised Land, which once was forbidden him, and talks with Jesus on the Mount of Transfiguration. Our disappointments, which may seem

[1] Cecil Frances Alexander, "Burial of Moses."

to us complete frustration and failure, lead us on to greater things and certify to us the life to come. Disappointment is like a sieve. Through the meshes of the sieve the coarse and base things fall to the ground, while the golden grain remains. Not seldom a great disappointment has transformed a selfish and self-centered man into a man who delights to think and to do for others. The disappointment of Jehoshaphat in the great expedition which he had planned to go to a far-off land to bring back the gold of Ophir made him a better king. There is no record of his again making an alliance with one of the wicked kings of Israel, and in that way helping the ungodly. When the ships of your fondest desires and dreams and ambitions are broken on the rocks, do not despair, but look for some good purpose in God's providence. Have faith that he is able to give you something far better than the gold of Ophir; things that "eye hath not seen, nor ear heard, neither have entered into the heart of man." And that "something" is eternal life through eternal ages in Jesus Christ.

IV

SEVEN WHO SAID NO

How to Refuse Evil

> "The child shall know to refuse the evil." Isa. 7:16

IN ISAIAH'S BEAUTIFUL DESCRIPTION OF THE MESSIAH, the Saviour of the world, occurs this striking phrase: "The child shall know to refuse the evil." To be able to know the difference between good and evil, to have the will and the power to refuse the evil, has ever been true of great characters. As a general thing, we lay the emphasis upon what men do or allow or permit; but what men refuse to do is a vital factor in the building of strong character. Morally great men, from Abraham up to the Son of man, were men who knew how to "refuse the evil."

JOSEPH

One of the most celebrated of those who knew how to refuse the evil, and did refuse it, was Joseph. The turning point in Joseph's life was his temptation in the house of Potiphar. Upon the refusal that he then made rose the structure of his magnificent character. Sold as a slave into Egypt by his cruel brethren, because of their envy of him, Joseph had been bought by Potiphar, the captain of Pharaoh's guard. There his ability, his friendly disposition, and his industry soon won high promotion for him. He was made overseer of Potiphar's house, and all the business of this high officer was committed to Joseph's hand. The sun of prosperity was shining kindly upon him, and Joseph was on the way to still higher rank.

Then suddenly came the temptation by Potiphar's wife, a beautiful, but wicked woman. From the standpoint of the world, and of the customs of Egypt, everything was on the side of Joseph's yielding to that temptation. In the first place, he was far from home and his father's house. The standards of Egypt were quite different from those of Israel. In Egypt there were no Ten Commandments. The God of Israel had permitted him to be sold as a slave into Egypt. Why then should he be faithful to that God? There was the urge of youth and the flame of his passions. To yield was the gateway to promotion; he would have a friend at court. But to refuse meant loss of his position, and his life would be in jeopardy, for "hell hath no fury like a woman scorned." And yet Joseph refused. How did he come to do that? How did he come to make that decision which has made his name immortal? Because, like Moses, he "saw him who is invisible." What he said to the temptress, and what he said to his own soul, too, was this: "How can I do this great wickedness, and sin against God?"

The result of his refusal was a false and wicked accusation. He was cast into the darkness of Pharaoh's dungeon, where, as the Psalmist said of him centuries later, the "iron entered into his soul." [1] But after the record of how Joseph was cast into prison comes this mighty and glorious sentence, "But the Lord was with Joseph!" He had refused to do evil, to sin against God, and by so doing had, apparently, lost every chance of promotion and honor in Egypt. But that is not the end of the story. The end of the story is that God, who was with Joseph, delivered him out of the prison. He was promoted to be the prime minister of Egypt, and in that high post he was able by his wise measures to save Egypt from starvation, and, in the providence of God, his own people and nation. Pharaoh's gold chain, we are told, was put about Joseph's neck. Once in the museum at Cairo I saw a beautiful silver and gold ornament which had belonged to the Pharaoh of Joseph's day. If that gold chain which Pharaoh put about Joseph's neck is ever found, you will see engraved on it one word—"No!"

DANIEL

Seven centuries after Joseph, in another world empire, there was another young man whose name lives forever because he too knew how to refuse the evil. Daniel was one of a group of four young men who had been carried down from Jerusalem as captives, to be brought up at the court of the world despot, Nebuchadnezzar, the king of Babylon. The first thing that was done there was to change the names of these four young men from their Jewish names to Babylonian names. Hananiah became Shadrach;

[1] Ps. 105:18, *The Book of Common Prayer.*

Mishael became Meshach; Azariah became Abednego; and Daniel became Belteshazzar. The king of Babylon was able to change the name of Daniel; but, as we shall see, he was not able to change his principles.

The first thing which confronted Daniel and his companions was the invitation that came to them to sit at the king's table and partake of the king's food. This raised the problem of conscience, for on that table there was meat which was forbidden by the law of Moses and wine which had been offered as a sacrifice before the heathen altars. What now were these four young men to do?

I can imagine a discussion among them as they were dressing for dinner on that first evening. I can imagine Shadrach saying to Daniel and the other two: "Let us remember that we are far from home. We shall probably never see Jerusalem again. The best plan for us will be to do in Babylon as the Babylonians do. They eat different food here, and we can can hardly be expected to obey the Jewish traditions in that respect." Then, perhaps, Meshach added his word: "After all," he said, "right or wrong does not lie in what we eat or drink, but in what we do. Suppose this food has been offered to an idol? What difference does that make to us? We know that there is only one true God, and that an idol is nothing at all." Then Abednego added his word: "Remember," he said, "that we stand here at the gate of opportunity and promotion; everything is favorable for us. It would be foolish to lose our chance for distinction and high office in the empire of Babylon merely for a scruple about not eating the flesh of swine or drinking wine offered to Babylon's god. Why for the sake of this should we lose our chance, forfeit the favor of the king, and perhaps lose life itself?"

But Daniel said, "No; I will not eat of the king's meat." His mind had already been made up; he had prepared himself against the day of this temptation. Daniel "purposed in his heart that he would not defile himself with the portion of the king's meat, nor with the wine which he drank." Too often, young men lose their battle with the world before it is really commenced, because they have not purposed in their heart to stand alone and "refuse the evil." The upshot of this stand by Daniel was that he and his three companions were permitted to eat the Hebrew fare; and, doing so, they grew in body, in knowledge and learning, and in wisdom, and in favor with God and man.

That was the trial and temptation of Daniel's youth. Upon that refusal to eat the king's meat rose the structure of his magnificent and influential life, for he served as prime minister in the successive reigns of Nebuchadnezzar, Belshazzar, clear down to the reign of Darius. It was when he was an old man, in the reign of Darius, that Daniel's greatest trial befell him. But the boy of the reign of Nebuchadnezzar was father to the man.

When Daniel's enemies persuaded King Darius to issue a decree that for thirty days no one should offer a petition or make a prayer save to the king himself, their purpose was to secure the downfall of Daniel, for they were convinced that he would not obey such a decree and would continue to pray to the God of Israel as he had always done. Nor were they mistaken about the character of Daniel. I can imagine these conspirators on the first morning after the decree had been issued and posted throughout the city and throughout the land, discussing, as they lay hidden in the garden of Daniel's palace, whether or not he would disobey the king's decree. As the day dawned over the tawny Euphrates, and the mists began to lift, they could see the window of Daniel's palace. They knew it was at that window that he was wont to pray daily, opening the window toward Jerusalem. But now, as minutes passed by and the casement was not thrown open, there was some doubt among these conspirators as to whether their plot was going to succeed. "Hark!" one of them said to his fellows. "Do you hear that noise? It is the roar of the famished lions in their den. Daniel too has heard that noise, and he is no fonder of a lion's den than you and I are." Then, as they were waiting, slowly the casement was pushed open, and the aged statesman and servant of God knelt down, stretched out his arms toward Jerusalem, and prayed to the God of Abraham, Isaac, and Jacob.

The sun in heaven that morning looked down on no grander sight than Daniel, who refused to stop praying to the God of Israel, even though the punishment was to be cast into the den of the lions. And into that den he was cast. But in the morning, when King Darius, troubled in conscience, arose from a sleepless bed and went in haste to the den of lions, he looked down into that den and cried out, "O Daniel, servant of the living God, is thy God, whom thou servest continually, able to deliver thee from the lions?" And back from the depths of the lions' den came the answer of Daniel, "O king, live for ever. My God hath

55

sent his angel, and hath shut the lions' mouths, that they have not hurt me: forasmuch as before him innocency was found in me." He might have added, "And because I refused to obey the decree of Darius to stop praying."

THREE YOUNG MEN

Nor, among the great refusals of the past, must we forget that of Daniel's three companions. For some reason Daniel was not subjected to their fiery trial. Yet I have no doubt that it was the example of Daniel, when he refused to eat the king's meat, which inspired their great refusal and their magnificent stand for conscience and for God.

In his vainglory, Nebuchadnezzar had set up on the plains of Dura a great image of gold. For the dedication of this colossal image the satraps and rulers and chief men of all the provinces of the empire had assembled. To them the herald of the king made the royal proclamation, that at the sound of the cornet, flute, harp, sackbut, psaltery, dulcimer, and all kinds of music, everyone should fall on his face and worship the image that the king had set up. Whoever failed to do so was to be cast into the midst of a burning fiery furnace.

At the appointed time, when the music rang out over the plains of Dura, everyone, from the highest to the lowest, fell on his face before the golden image—all but three —Shadrach, Meshach, and Abednego. They refused to fall down and worship because they had been brought up on the Second Commandment, which forbade them to make any graven image or to bow down before it. This refusal of the three young men to bow down to his image was reported to the king, and when the king called the three youths to account, they said to him, "Our God whom we serve is able to deliver us from the burning fiery furnace, O king. But if not, be it known unto thee, O king, that we will not serve thy gods, nor worship the golden image which thou hast set up."

In his rage the king commanded that the furnace should be heated seven times more than it was usually heated, and that the three youths should be cast into the midst of this flaming furnace. When this had been done, it was reported to the king that the young men had not been harmed. In wonder and astonishment Nebuchadnezzar hastened to the furnace. After he had taken one look, he said to his counselors, "Did not we cast three men bound into the midst of the fire?" They answered and said unto the king, "True, O king." Then the king replied, "Lo, I see four men loose, walking in the midst of the fire, and they have no hurt; and the form of the fourth is like the Son of God."

The form of the fourth! And this form of the fourth was like unto the Son of God. The ancient promise of the God of Israel was, "When thou passest through the waters, I will be with thee; and through the rivers, they shall not overflow thee: . . . neither shall the flame kindle upon thee." Now that promise had been fulfilled. The grandeur of the refusal of these three Hebrew lads to bow down before Nebuchadnezzar's golden colossus lay in the fact of their faith, and their trust in the providence of God. When threatened with the fiery furnace, they said

57

to the king, "Our God whom we serve is able to deliver us from the burning fiery furnace, . . . O king. *But if not,* be it known unto thee, O king, that we will not serve thy gods nor worship the golden image." When commanded to "turn or burn," to bow down or be cast into the furnace seven times heated, they expressed a sublime faith in the providence of God. God was able to deliver them, if he so willed. But even if that were not his will, and even if they burned to ashes in that furnace, they would not forsake their God. They were ready to die as martyrs to their conscience. They were able to say what Job said in the midst of his great sufferings, "Though he slay me, yet will I trust him!"

No one, I suppose, has been able to locate the plain of Dura where that golden image was set up. Yet morally, spiritually, it is not hard to locate. You can find the plain of Dura and the golden image wherever men are called upon to choose between this world and the fear of God, between pleasure and conscience. That golden image may stand on the counter of a store, or in a quiet study, or in the preacher's pulpit. It may be set up in the lecture room of the college, on the playing field, in the halls of legislature, or in the quiet of one's secret chamber. There is spoken the same command, and there is uttered the same threat. There, too, burns the fiery furnace. But there, too, when the soul is faithful unto God, and makes the great refusal because of the fear of God, because it sees him who is invisible, there too will be seen, as in the experience of those three young men, the form of the fourth, like unto the Son of God.

VASHTI

In this roll call of those who made a great refusal, who knew how to refuse the evil, and whose names live forever, there is one name, the name of a woman, which ought not to be omitted. The name of this woman is Vashti, queen of Persia. For seven days and seven nights the despot of the world, Ahasuerus, king of Persia, had staged a great banquet in the palace at Shushan for the princes and nobles of the 127 provinces of his empire. It was a scene of splendor and magnificence such as only an oriental kingdom could display. In the great banqueting hall of the palace, washed by the waters of the River Ulai, Ahasuerus and his lords and nobles had been feasting and drinking for seven days and seven nights. The banqueting hall was adorned with great banners and streamers of white, green, and blue, caught with cords of fine linen and purple to silver rings in pillars of marble. The couches on which the guests reclined were of gold and silver, resting upon a tessellated pavement of red, blue, white, and black marble. Fountains flung their silver sprays toward the roof of the banqueting hall. There was music by the dulcimer, the harp, the cornet, the sackbut, and all the instruments known to the empire. Day after day, night after night, acrobats and jugglers and dancers had played their part, and successive pantomimes had entertained the revelers. But on this last night came the climax—the great sensation. It was the inspiration of the drunken brain of Ahasuerus. Suddenly the king bethought himself of his beautiful queen, Vashti. "The queen!" he said to himself. "I will bring her in and display her charms to my nobles and lords and captains!" Summoning his seven chamberlains, he said to them, "Bring in the queen, that she may display herself before me and my nobles!" When the half-drunken revelers heard this, they were at first shocked, but after the first moment of surprise and shock, they were delighted and cried out, "Yes! The queen! Bring in the queen!"

After a little the great crimson curtains at one end of the hall parted, and the chief of the chamberlains entered with an anxious and troubled look upon his countenance. Approaching Ahasuerus, he whispered to him, "The queen refuses to come in!" The countenance of the king grew white with anger. Yet he knew that he could not compel her to come in, and the eager and drunken banqueters were disappointed in their expectation and desire.

"But the queen Vashti refused to come at the king's commandment." It cost her her crown. She was removed from the throne and shut up in lonely solitude for the rest of her days. But she had saved the honor of her soul. The crown of gold and precious stones fell from her beautiful head, but it remained upon her soul. She refused to come in! Searching amid the dust heaps of Shushan, I came upon a flaming jewel. Engraven upon it was this sentence, "But the Queen Refused." Great is the influence of women who do not go around with the crowd and do as the world does, but stand for God and conscience. The secret of strength of character lies not only in a readiness to receive and choose the good, but in the power to refuse the evil. Woman's influence is powerful because it is strategic, for she acts at the sources of human conduct. In

Measure for Measure the beautiful Isabella was tempted to procure the release of her brother, who had been sentenced to death, but at the price of selling her virtue. When she refused this temptation, the tempter said to her, "Then must your brother die!" Whereupon Isabella, knowing how to refuse the evil, made her great answer:

> Better it were a brother dies at once,
> Than that a sister, by redeeming him,
> Should die for ever.

JESUS

At the head of the holy procession of those who knew how to refuse evil always marches the Son of God. When we speak of him, we lay the emphasis upon his deeds, his words, his sacrificial death on the cross. But let us not forget his *refusals*. It was of him whose name is Immanuel, the Prince of Heaven, but born of a virgin, that it was said, "The child shall know to refuse the evil." There were many great refusals in the life and ministry of our Lord; but the refusal upon which the character of the Redeemer was built was when, at the very beginning of his ministry, he was tempted by the devil. In his *Paradise Regained,* John Milton properly commences with the temptation of Jesus, for it was that refusal, and that victory over the temptation of the devil, which qualified Jesus to become our Saviour.

He was "led up of the spirit into the wilderness to be tempted of the devil." It was necessary to discover whether or not he knew "how to refuse the evil." When he was hungry after a forty-day fast, and all of his physical nature was craving food, the devil came to him and asked him to turn stones into bread; but Jesus refused to do so. He refused to depart from God's appointed plan for him by working a miracle, and said to the tempter, "Man shall not live by bread alone, but by every word that proceedeth out of the mouth of God."

In the second temptation the devil took him up to a pinnacle of the Temple and, quoting the ninety-first psalm, which says, "He shall give his angels charge over thee. . . . They shall bear thee up in their hands, lest thou dash thy foot against a stone," asked him to cast himself down from the pinnacle. The inference of this temptation was that he would win recognition as the Messiah by the performance of so dazzling a miracle. But Jesus said to him, "It is written, Thou shalt not tempt the Lord thy God."

Then came the third temptation, when the devil took him up into an exceeding high mountain, and showed him all the kingdoms of the world, and the glory of them, and said unto him, "All these things will I give thee, if thou wilt fall down and worship me." But Jesus refused to do this great evil, and said to the tempter, "Get thee hence, Satan: for it is written, Thou shalt worship the Lord thy God, and him only shalt thou serve."

The three temptations were all different; yet they were all alike in this—that they involved a departure from the will of God. And that is what sin always is—departing from the will of God.

Thus it is that souls are made great. They qualify to

save themselves and others by refusing to do the evil. The greatest refusal of Jesus came in Gethsemane's shadows, when he knelt and prayed, under a final temptation of the devil, "If it be possible, let this cup pass from me: nevertheless not as I will, but as thou wilt." Then on the cross, when Satan tempted him again through the priests and scribes and people and thieves, who cried out, "If thou be the Son of God, come down from the cross," Jesus refused. He "saw the travail of his soul and was satisfied." He *endured, as seeing him who is invisible.* Upon that refusal rests the world's redemption.

To every dark spirit of temptation, to every tempter disguised as an angel of light, to every suggestion to put the body above the soul, to serve time rather than eternity, thou shalt learn how to refuse. Thou shalt say, "No!" But there is One whom it is life to obey, and death to refuse. It is he who refused for our sake to do evil. He stands now before you. Hear him, "Behold, I stand at the door, and knock: if any man hear my voice, and open the door, I will come in to him, and will sup with him, and he with me."

To him never say, "No!" To him thou shalt say, "Yes!" Perhaps up to this time you have said "No" to him. But that "No" need not be final. Still he waits for your answer. To say "Yes" to him means life eternal. To say "Yes" to him will enroll you as a citizen of the commonwealth of the redeemed, the first born, whose names are written in heaven.

V

ONESIPHORUS
A Friend in Chains

"And was not ashamed of my chain."
II Tim. 1 :16

THERE WERE SOME OF PAUL'S FRIENDS WHO WERE
ashamed of his chain. In the day of danger and adversity
they forsook him. But not this faithful friend from
Ephesus.

Chains are the test of friendship. They show whether
it is just a fair-weather friendship or a friendship born
for adversity. Those who wrote the ancient fables were
great preachers. One of the famous fables was that of
the two travelers and the bear. On their journey the travelers suddenly encountered a bear. One in great fear immediately climbed into a tree and hid himself, without a
thought of his companion. The other, with no chance to
go anywhere, and having heard that a bear will not touch
a dead body, threw himself on the ground and pretended
to be dead. The bear came up and began to nuzzle him and
sniff at his nose and mouth and ears, and, thinking him
dead, went off.

When the bear was out of sight, the one who had
climbed the tree came down, and asked his friend what it
was that the bear had whispered to him, "for," he said,

"I noticed that he put his mouth very close to your ear." The other said: "It was no great secret that he told me. What he said was to have a care how I kept company with those who, when trouble or danger arises, desert their friends and leave them in the lurch."

The old fables strike true and ever-resounding chords of human experience and relationship; and never more so than this fable of the two travelers and the bear. Paul had many friends, and warm friends. Let no one think of the Apostle as pure and cold intellect. He did indeed have a great mind; but his heart was still greater. Chrysostom, the golden-mouthed preacher of Antioch, in what is perhaps the greatest tribute ever written of Paul, at the end of his sermons on the Letter to the Romans, says that of all the cities of the world he loves Rome most, not because the great Caesars reigned there, but because Paul died there, and there he could see "the dust of that heart which a man would not do wrong to call the heart of the world; so enlarged that it could take in cities and nations and peoples; a heart which burned at each one that was lost; which despised both death and hell; and yet was broken down by a brother's tears."

PAUL'S FRIENDS

Among the friends of Paul whom he names and salutes in his letters was Mark, who had failed in his first relationship with Paul, and whom, because he had deserted him and turned back at Perga on the first missionary journey, Paul would not permit to accompany him on the second journey. Afterward, given a second chance, Mark "made good." At the very end of his life, Paul, in his last letter to Timothy, asks him to bring Mark with him, "for he is profitable to me for the ministry."

Others of Paul's friends were: Silas, who went with him on the second journey; and Onesimus, the fugitive slave of Philemon, converted by Paul at Rome; and Epaphroditus, the friend from the church at Philippi who came to see Paul when he was a prisoner at Rome; and Priscilla and Aquila, who risked their lives to help him; and Titus, who brought him comforting news about the church at Corinth; and Tychicus, the "beloved brother," who carried Paul's letters to the Ephesians and the Colossians; and Tertius, his amanuensis, who took down by dictation the Letter to the Romans; and Amplias, "beloved in the Lord"; and Timothy, "my beloved son"; the friend whom Paul at the very end wanted to come to him at Rome, and to "come before winter"; and last, but not least, Luke, the "beloved physician," whom Paul hands down to immortality with that imperishable encomium, "Only Luke is with me." What a list of friends were on Paul's prayer calendar, and he on theirs!

Not all of Paul's friends, however, were faithful. Before we come to this beautiful mention of Onesiphorus, Paul writes: "This thou knowest, that all they which are in Asia be turned away from me; of whom are Phygellus and Hermogenes." That is all we know of these two friends, who, together with others from the province of Asia, forsook Paul when he was in trouble and in prison. Another friend who was not faithful to the end was Demas, perhaps from the church at Thessalonica, of whom Paul writes, "Demas hath forsaken me, having loved this present world." In two earlier letters Paul had sent the salutations of Demas with his own to the disciples at Colosse and Philippi.

In contrast with these friends who forsook him in his hour of need, Paul writes this beautiful word about Onesiphorus, the friend from Ephesus, who came to see him when he was in prison at Rome:

The Lord give mercy unto the house of Onesiphorus; for he oft refreshed me, and was not ashamed of my chain: but, when he was in Rome, he sought me out very diligently, and found me. The Lord grant unto him that he may find mercy of the Lord in that day: and in how many things he ministered unto me at Ephesus, thou knowest very well.

PRAYERS FOR THE DEAD

Before we go further in this story of a friend who was not afraid or ashamed of chains, we mention in passing that these words about Onesiphorus, perhaps the only ones in the Bible, are frequently appealed to as scriptural warrant for prayers for the dead. It is pointed out that Paul asks mercy for the *house*—that is, the family—of Onesiphorus; and that when he does ask mercy to Onesiphorus; it is that he may "find mercy of the Lord in that day"—that is, the day of judgment.

We cannot be certain from the reading of Paul's reference to Onesiphorus that this Ephesian friend was dead. Perhaps he was with Paul at Rome when the letter was written, and that is why Paul asks the great blessing of God's mercy upon his family. Nor because Paul expresses the pious desire that Onesiphorus may find mercy in the day of judgment, does it necessarily follow that he was dead. Long before any controversy arose between Catholics and Protestants over prayers for the dead, ancient Church fathers, Thodoret and Chrysostom among them, held the view that Onesiphorus was living when Paul wrote the Letter to Timothy.

But whether Onesiphorus was living or dead, all that Paul asks is that his great kindness to him when he was in prison shall not be forgotten in the day of judgment, when the books are opened. We can be sure that it will be remembered, for in his great preview of the judgment Jesus said that the King will say to those on his right hand: "I was an hungred, and ye gave me meat: I was thirsty, and ye gave me drink: I was a stranger, and ye took me in: naked, and ye clothed me: I was sick, and ye visited me: I was in prison, and ye came unto me. . . . Inasmuch as ye have done it unto one of the least of these my brethren, ye have done it unto me." This, after all, is the great thing to remember here, and the great and beautiful thing to imitate, that to show mercy to those in distress is pleasing to God and will not go unremembered.

The logic of the gospel is against prayers for the dead, certainly the elaborated machinery of prayers for the dead which finds expression in masses for the dead. The salvation of the soul rests upon the great work of Christ on the cross for sinners, not upon the prayers of even the most pious and devout. Jesus said to the dying robber, "Today shalt thou be with me in paradise." What more than that could we ask for, if we did pray for the dead? If they are with Christ in paradise, they need no prayer from us.

But because we do not pray for the dead, nor find in the Bible any ground for doing so, it does not follow that we dismiss the beloved dead from our thought. By no means. If one has for years prayed for a dear child, or parent, or brother or sister, or husband or wife, or friend, will he suddenly cease to think of them, or make mention of them before God? Certainly not.

I have loved ones in the King's country, and I frequently mention their names in my prayers. But in this way: I pray that the memory of them, the faith and Christlike spirit which were in them, shall influence my own life and make me like them. Thus it is that the dead live again in lives made better by the thought of them.

ONESIPHORUS AND PAUL'S CHAIN

It was dangerous for Christians at Rome to let it be known that they were the friends of Paul the prisoner. As we have seen, many could not meet that test of friendship and fell away from Paul. Not so Onesiphorus. We gather from the narrative that Onesiphorus had difficulty in finding where Paul was imprisoned, for Paul says, "He sought me out *very diligently,* and found me." Some would not have searched at all; others would have satisfied their conscience with just one effort, and then abandoned the quest. But Onesiphorus kept searching until he found Paul; and when he found him, he cheered him and refreshed him.

Can you not see Onesiphorus, with a basket on his arm,

perhaps a newly woven robe, too, going here and there in Rome—to the market place, amid the throng at the Forum, at the Capitoline Hill, and at the palace and the barracks—seeking for Paul, and sometimes roughly and rudely and threateningly repulsed by the guards and the soldiers? Yet the kind, noble, and courageous soul did not give up the search. Perhaps it was days or months before he located Paul in that vast and crowded city. And can you not see him as, having found Paul, he took out of his basket those refreshments and that robe, and handed them over to Paul, and then told him news of Timothy and the church at Ephesus? And all the little kindnesses he showed him, as long as the guards permitted him to visit the jail?

In *Great Expectations,* Charles Dickens tells how the boy Pip went to visit for the last time his benefactor, Magwitch, the dying convict, who had been condemned to be hanged. The convict took Pip's hand and said: "You've never deserted me, dear boy. . . . And what's best of all, you've been more comfortable alonger me since I was under a dark cloud than when the sun shone. That's best of all." Yes; it is not when the sun is shining, but when the clouds gather, and darkness comes down, and our friend wears a chain, that friendship comes to its most beautiful flower.

Sir Philip Sidney, poet, philosopher, and soldier of the sixteenth century, fell in battle on the field of Zutphen in 1586. In his great distress he called for a drink of water; but as he was putting the cup to his lips, he saw near him another dying man whose eyes were fixed longingly on the cup. Lowering his hand, Sidney handed him the cup, saying, "Thy necessity is greater than mine." Acts like that have made his name immortal for kindness and grace. It was not strange, therefore, that a knight of that age asked that this epitaph be put upon his grave: "Here lies the friend of Sir Philip Sidney." If you had asked Onesiphorus what epitaph he desired, I am sure he would have said, "Here lies the friend of Paul." But if you had asked Paul to write the epitaph for Onesiphorus, I am sure it would have been this: "Here lies one who was not ashamed of my chain."

The man who wrote the following lines, whoever he was, wrote on the assumption that Onesiphorus was dead when Paul mentioned him in his Letter to Timothy. As we have seen, this is not a necessary assumption. Nevertheless, these lines on Onesiphorus bring out for us the beautiful deed of Onesiphorus, and how Paul repaid that deed with prayer and gratitude:

> Timotheus, when here and there you go
> Through Ephesus upon your pastoral round,
> Where every street to me is hallowed ground,
> I will be bold and ask you to bestow
> Kindness upon one home, where long ago
> A helpmate lived, whose like is seldom found;
> And when the sweet spring flowers begin to blow,
> Sometime for me, lay one upon his mound.[1]

One of the many shameful things that Jean Jacques Rousseau relates of himself in his celebrated *Confessions* is his reaction when, as he and his companion, with whom

---

[1] Author unknown.

he had been wandering over France, reached Lyons, his friend had an attack of epilepsy on the public square. Rousseau, instead of going to his succor, fled from the scene and abandoned him to the mercy of strangers. He was ashamed of his chain. If to do that is base and ignoble, to help a friend in chains is the mark of a noble character.

When Martin Luther was entering the bishop's palace at Worms to answer before the emperor and the Diet, and there make his great stand for Christ and for truth, an old knight clapped him on the shoulder and said: "My dear monk, my poor monk, thou art going to make such a stand as neither I nor any of my companions in arms have ever made in our hottest battles. If thou art sure of the justice of thy cause, then forward in God's name, and be of good courage! God will not forsake thee!" He was not ashamed of Luther's chain.

Years ago in Philadelphia a bank failed. There had been dishonesty on the part of some connected with the bank. Among others, a shadow had fallen, unjustly, over the name of an officer of the bank, who was also prominent in church affairs. One morning he received a letter. When he opened it, he saw just one sheet of paper. On the sheet was drawn a man's hand, and under the hand the name of one of his friends.

A verse in Proverbs says: "A friend loveth at all times, and a brother is born for adversity." Alas, there are many friends, fair-weather friends, who are not born for adversity. Adversity is the wind which separates the chaff of flattery from the grain of real friendship. The Shadow once said to the Body: "Who is a friend like me?

I follow you wherever you go. In sunlight or in moonlight I never forsake you." "True," replied the Body. "You go with me in sunlight and in moonlight. But where are you when neither sun nor moon shines upon me?"

The most beautiful illustration of our theme, the faithful and unashamed friend, is the story of David and Jonathan. David was the natural and inevitable rival for the throne to Saul's son, Jonathan. Yet Jonathan "stripped himself" for the sake of David, and said to him, "Thou shalt be king over Israel, and I shall be next unto thee." Although he risked his own life, he did not forsake David in the day of his adversity, when he was pursued by the jealous rage of Saul. How pleasing is that incident in the wood of Ziph! David, pursued by Saul, was hiding with his companions in the forest of Ziph. From what follows, we know that he was beginning to lose heart, and his faith in God was shaken. That night Jonathan, with great peril to himself, left the lines of Saul's army and went over to David in the wood of Ziph, and there "strengthened his hand in God." That is the highest service one friend can do for another—strengthen his hand in God in the day of adversity. Jonathan was not ashamed of David's chain. No wonder that when he heard of Jonathan's death in battle on Mount Gilboa, David exclaimed, "Thy love to me was wonderful, passing the love of women!"

THE FRIEND ABOVE ALL FRIENDS

Onesiphorus was a faithful and unashamed friend to Paul because both of them were friends of the Friend that sticketh closer than a brother. Not many of us can have a friend like Paul to whom to minister, and not many, either, in the dark hours of life can have a friend like Onesiphorus to minister to us. No; I take that back. We all have that greatest of all friends, the Friend of friends, the "Friend of sinners." That Friend is never ashamed of your chain. He is the one who never leaves and never forsakes you. "Greater love," said that Friend, "hath no man than this, that a man lay down his life for his friends." And he who said that, did that very thing. When we were lost and entangled in the wood and thicket of sin, he came to seek us and to strengthen our hand in God.

> Jesus sought me when a stranger,
>   Wand'ring from the fold of God;
> He, to rescue me from danger,
>   Interposed His precious blood.[2]

Onesiphorus, true and faithful friend, not ashamed of Paul's chain, and who didst seek and hunt for Paul there in ancient Rome, until thou hadst found him, and oft refreshed him, the very mention of thy name is like a cool, refreshing wind. Long since, we know, Paul's prayer for thee has been answered, and thou hast found mercy before God. May we too find that same sweet mercy. Inspire our hearts, Onesiphorus, to be the loving, faithful friend to those in chains, even as thou wast to Paul. May we never

[2] Robert Robinson.

be ashamed of our friends' chains, but ever refresh them, as thou didst Paul in his dungeon there at Rome. Thou friend of Paul, thou friend of Christ, wilt thou now permit us to call thee friend? And if, Onesiphorus, it be permitted to the souls in heaven to pray for those upon earth, then humbly we ask that as Paul prayed for thee, so thou wilt pray for us that we too may obtain mercy in "that day."

VI

FIVE DRUNKARDS OF
THE BIBLE

Five Famous Preachers

> "At the last it biteth like a serpent,
> and stingeth like an adder."
>
> Prov. 23:32

THERE ARE DIFFERENT WAYS OF PREACHING A SERMON on the subject of intemperance and the terrible ravages of strong drink. One way, which is somewhat popular today, is to show the fearful economic waste of the liquor habit and the liquor business, the price the nation must pay in the maintenance of the hospitals, prisons, penitentiaries, poor houses, and asylums for the insane. Another way is to show how strong drink is the great killer, by accidents on the highways and through the destruction of the organs of the drinker's body. Oliver Wendell Holmes summed this up when he said that alcohol destroys men's viscera when they are alive and preserves them when they were dead. Another way is to get the records of the magistrates' courts and the police records and the criminal courts and show the vast amount of crime that is traceable to strong drink. But, after all, man's soul is the important and the immortal part of man. I therefore choose to emphasize how strong drink does injury to the souls of men. And instead

76

of preaching a sermon myself, I shall call upon five drunkards of the Bible and let them do the preaching.

NOAH

I was the son of Lamech and the grandson of Methuselah. When I was born, my father called me Noah, saying, "He shall comfort us concerning our work and toil of our hands, because of the ground which the Lord hath cursed." Little could my father have foreseen in how wonderful a way I was to comfort the the earth, because by the will and plan of God I was the man who saved the human race from destruction.

When I came to manhood, there was great wickedness in the earth, and every imagination of the thought of man's heart was only evil continually. It repented the Lord that he had made man on the earth, and it grieved him at his heart. And the Lord said, "I will destroy man whom I have created from the face of the earth." But I found grace in the eyes of the Lord.

One day the Lord spoke to me and said, "The end of all flesh is come before me." All flesh had corrupted his way upon the earth. God then gave me directions to build a great ark, saying that he would bring a flood of waters upon the earth, but that I and my family—for I had three sons, Ham, Shem, and Japheth—would be saved alive in the ark.

I obeyed the word of the Lord and began to build the ark. Men laughed at me and scoffed, and, looking up at the cloudless sky, said, "Where is the sign of this great rain and flood that you say is coming, Noah?" But I went on with my work and finished the ark. Then God broke up the fountains of the great deep, and the windows of heaven were opened, and there was rain upon the earth forty days and forty nights, and the waters prevailed exceedingly. The whole earth was covered, and all the high hills were covered, and all flesh died.

At the end of 150 days the waters began to assuage, and the tops of the highest mountains were seen. I opened the window of the ark and let out a raven, which went to and fro, but did not return to the ark, for the raven could live on floating carrion. Then I sent forth a dove, but the dove found no rest for the sole of its foot and came back to the ark. After another seven days I sent forth a dove again. Ere long she came back with an olive leaf in her mouth. Then I knew that the flood was over.

When the ark grounded at the foot of a high mountain, I went forth with my wife and my three sons and their wives. The first thing I did was to build an altar unto the Lord. The Lord was pleased with my sacrifice, and said that he would not again destroy the earth with a flood, and while the earth remained, seedtime and harvest, cold and heat, summer and winter, day and night, should never cease. As a beautiful pledge of his covenant, he set the rainbow in the cloud.

After the flood was over, I planted a vineyard. With the first ripe grapes I made wine. It was sweet to my taste, after long abstinence on the ark. I drank, and drank, and drank again; and was drunken. I lost all consciousness and lay sprawled on the ground, naked and uncovered before my family. Two of my sons, Shem and Japheth, took a garment and laid it upon their shoulders and went backward, and covered the nakedness of their father, for they could not bear to look upon me in that drunken and shameful state.

Who would have thought that I, the same Noah who had found grace in the sight of the Lord, to whom God spoke, who saved the human race by obeying the word of the Lord, am the man who lay there drunken, uncovered, and naked before his sons?

The Bible speaks of me as the man who "by faith, being warned of God of things not seen as yet, moved with fear, prepared an ark to the saving of his house; by the which he condemned the world, and became heir of the righteousness which is by faith." The apostle Peter calls me "a preacher of righteousness." Yet I can never forget that terrible day when I awoke out of my drunkenness and found myself naked and uncovered on the ground. I was, indeed, a preacher of righteousness when I warned men of the flood and told them to come into the ark; but I am also a preacher of righteousness because by my drunkenness I warn men, and even those who stand high, and do the work of the Lord, against the peril and danger of strong drink. I say to men that

> The gray-haired saint may fall at last;
> The surest guide a wanderer prove.
> Death only binds us fast
> To that bright shore of love.[1]

[1] Author unknown.

Strong drink has claimed many a victim; but I, Noah, the first drunkard, more than any other, show and illustrate in my own fall what strong drink can do to the soul of man.

LOT

I was the nephew of Abraham. I had the great advantage of his companionship and friendship. Through him I prospered and had many tents and flocks and herds. But there arose strife between the herdmen of Abraham and my herdmen. My uncle Abraham took me one day to the top of a high hill and said to me, "Let there be no strife, I pray thee, between me and thee, and between my herdmen and thy herdmen; for we be brethren. Is not the whole land before thee? separate thyself, I pray thee, from me: if thou wilt take the left hand, then I will go to the right; or if thou depart to the right hand, then I will go to the left."

Abraham was my uncle. It was through his kindness that I had prospered. I ought to have said to him, "Abraham, thou art the friend of God and the father of the faithful. It is not for me to choose, but for thee. Choose thou the best part of the land, and I will take what is left." But in my selfishness and greed I availed myself of his generous offer. Lifting up my eyes, I beheld all the plain of Jordan toward the south, that it was well watered like the Garden of the Lord. That was the portion of land which I chose. I knew that the wicked cities of the plain, Sodom and Gomorrah, were located there. But that did not keep me from choosing that land, for I was eager to become as rich and great as Abraham.

It was not my intention to become an inhabitant of Sodom. At the first I only pitched my tent toward Sodom; but before long, I found myself dwelling in Sodom. My daughters had married men of Sodom, and I was on the town council, sitting at the gate. I prospered exceedingly; but I thought that I could have worldly prosperity without danger to my soul or to my family. I received one warning when the king of Elam, Chedorlaomer, and three other kings, fought against the king of Sodom and four other kings with him in the vale of Siddim. The four kings defeated the five kings; Sodom was taken and looted, and I was carried off with the other prisoners when the army of the king of Elam withdrew to the east. I was rescued out of my captivity by my uncle Abraham, who risked his life to save mine. But this experience did not persuade me to get out of Sodom.

Then one evening two men, who proved to be angels, appeared at my door in Sodom. They told me that God would destroy the place, because the cry of it had waxed great before the face of the Lord. They said to me to take my wife and my daughters and my sons-in-law and flee the wicked city. When the morning came, I went out to get my daughters and to warn my sons-in-law. But when I warned them and told them what the angels had said, they laughed at me; I seemed unto them "as one that mocked"; and no wonder, for I had not warned them against their evil ways. Even at the very last, I was reluctant to leave the city, my beautiful home, and my prosperous business; and the angels had to take me by the hand and draw me out from my house. Ere long

the heavens were dark and filled with smoke, when the
Lord rained brimstone and fire upon Sodom and Gomorrah. The angels had said to me, "Look not behind thee, . . .
lest thou be consumed." But my wife, filled with curiosity,
and frightened, looked behind her, and was turned into
a pillar of salt.

At length I reached the town of Zoar, high up on the
mountain. I was afraid to stay in any house in the city,
but spent the night in a cave. Alas, my two daughters
plied me with drink! Thus, in shameful incest, I became
the father of two sons, Moab and Ammon, and they in
turn became the ancestors of the Ammonites and the
Moabites, inveterate enemies of the people of God, de-
nounced and cursed by all the prophets. That One whose
day Abraham saw, when his own day came, said, "Remember Lot's wife!" But I tell you to remember not
only Lot's wife, but to remember me! Remember Lot!
For when you remember me, you will think of the great
sin into which I fell when I was drunken. Peter calls
me "just Lot, vexed with the filthy conversation of the
wicked." He says, "That righteous man dwelling among
them, . . . vexed his righteous soul from day to day with
their unlawful deeds." But when I think of what befell
me when I lay drunken in that cave at Zoar, and all the
evil that came out of that through the Ammonites and
the Moabites, I feel that I am hardly worthy of the title
"just Lot." Once I was just, but strong drink overthrew
me. It is true that, sodden with drink, I knew not what
I did. I have had many descendants. All those who, called
before the judge in the criminal court and convicted of

murder or adultery or assault, and asked if they have anything to say before sentence is pronounced, make the plea that they did not know what they were doing because they were drunken, are my descendants.

BELSHAZZAR

I was a descendant of the great king Nebuchadnezzar, and I sat upon the throne of Babylon in splendor and glory. I was the master of the world. I had a wise mother, and the great prophet Daniel, who had served under Nebuchadnezzar, became my counselor. If I had followed his example, I would not have lost my throne. When he was a young man at Nebuchadnezzar's court, Daniel, asked to eat things forbidden by the law of Israel and to drink wine, refused. He would not defile himself. Would that I had followed his example!

But one evil night I gave a great banquet in my palace for a thousand of my lords and nobles, their ladies, their wives, and their concubines. From the windows of the palace gorgeous, golden banners floated softly in the evening breeze. The floor was of tessellated marble, white, red, black, and blue, and the walls were hung with tapestries on which were traced the winged symbols of Babylon's power and pomp. Candelabra from far-off Damascus swung from the ceilings, and golden candlesticks glowed with soft radiance on the tables. In the center of the hall fountains flung up their silver spray. Innumerable braziers filled the banqueting hall with the pleasant intoxication of sweet incense.

When the guests had all been seated, I came in with

my wives and concubines and took my seat at the elevated table. Every part of the realm had been ransacked for a contribution to that feast. When the banquet was well under way, and my nobles and I were heated with wine of all nations, then the dancing women from the Caucasus and from Syria entered, and in their filmy garments glided wantonly in and out among the tables of the drunken nobles. I and the thousand lords greeted their immodest performance with shouts of applause.

Then I remembered something. But would that I had forgotten it! I remembered that Nebuchadnezzar had brought down from Jerusalem the sacred vessels of the temple of Jehovah. In my drunken excitement the idea struck me, Why not bring in the sacred vessels of the Jews and drink our wine out of them? I gave the order to one of the eunuchs, and presently the golden vessels were brought in. When the banqueters saw them, and understood what I was going to do with them, they made the palace shake with their shouts of joy. Soon Jehovah's sacred vessels were smeared with the slaver of my drunken lords. And as they drank, they praised the gods of Babylon, the gods of gold and silver and iron and brass and wood and stone. What a joke to drink to the heathen gods out of the vessels dedicated to the worship of Jehovah! Standing up, and holding one of the vessels in my hand, I shouted, "Where now is the God of the Hebrews? Palsied be every tongue that will not drink to the gods of Belshazzar! Where is the God of the Hebrews?"

He was nearer than I or anyone else thought. Suddenly,

on the wall over against me, near the candlestick, illuminated by its sevenfold light, I saw to my horror the fingers of a man's hand—not the whole hand or arm—only the fingers—and the fingers were writing on the wall. When I saw that, my slavering lips trembled, my knees smote together in terror, and the holy vessel in my defiling hand fell with a loud crash on the marble pavement. This is what I saw but did not understand: *"Mene, Mene, Tekel, Upharsin!"* These were the words, but no one could understand them.

Then Daniel was brought in. Daniel did not attend such banquets. But when he was found, he came in and stood at my side. Daniel was then ninety years of age. What a contrast between him, with his white locks and God-fearing countenance, and the scene of drunkenness and debauchery, and now terror, upon which he looked! I asked him to interpret for me the words that the hand had written on the wall. This was the interpretation: *Mene*—"God hath numbered thy kingdom, and finished it." *Tekel*—"Thou art weighed in the balances, and art found wanting." *Peres*—"Thy kingdom is divided, and given to the Medes and Persians."

When Daniel pronounced these words of doom, there was silence in the banqueting hall. Then suddenly I heard the blast of a trumpet and the tramp of armed feet as the soldiers of Darius, the general of Cyrus, came charging up the marble stairway and burst into the banqueting hall. Swords flashed; curses, groans, shouts, vain pleas for mercy, rang through the hall. Trembling in terror, I saw a Persian soldier, his sword uplifted, coming toward me. I got to my feet and tried to usheathe my sword, but it fell from my palsied hand. Then the sword of the Persian passed through my body under the fifth rib, and I fell down among the thousand nobles and their women where they lay dead in the slush of mingled wine and blood.

> That night they slew him on his father's throne,
> He died unnoticed and the hand unknown,
> Crownless and sceptreless Belshazzar lay
> A robe of purple 'round a form of clay.[2]

Listen to my sermon. It was when I was drunk that I was moved to profane the holy vessels. My death that night is a warning to all drinkers not to profane holy things. God has told us that our body is a sacred vessel. "Know ye not that your body is the temple of the Holy Ghost?"

AMNON

I am Amnon. I was the son of David; Absalom was my half brother. One day, loafing and drinking in my palace, I saw the beautiful Tamar, Absalom's fair sister and my half sister, passing by. I conceived a guilty passion for Tamar. Yet conscience warned me, and my better self drew back in dread from what I desired to do. But I had a friend. Alas! how many have stained their souls and gone down to ruin because they had a friend, but the wrong kind of friend! David my father had a friend, but that friend was the noble Jonathan. Peter had a friend,

[2] Author unknown.

but that friend was John the beloved. Paul had a friend, but that friend was Luke the beloved. And I had a friend, but he was the wrong kind of friend. It was he who suggested to me the way in which I could accomplish my evil desire.

When the evil thing had been done, then I hated Tamar as fiercely as I had greatly loved her before. Despite her pleas I turned her out onto the street. Absalom, her brother, chanced to come by not long after, and saw Tamar lying there on the road with her garments rent and ashes on her head. He comforted her and lifted her up and carried her into his palace. Then did I greatly fear the wrath and vengeance of Absalom. Always when I went abroad, I was armed and had armed guards with me. Thus passed two full years. One day I received an invitation to join all the sons of David at the banquet in Absalom's palace at the time of the sheepshearing. This is always a time of merrymaking, of feasting, and of drinking. At first I was afraid to go. Then I remembered that two years had passed since my sin against Tamar. Perhaps, I thought to myself, the anger and wrath of Absalom will have subsided by this time. I was weary, too, of going about always armed and having armed men with me. So I went down to Baal-hazor to the feast of the sheepshearers. It was a great feast. There was a spitted ox and all kinds of wine. With the rest I drank deeply. All fear left me. I shouted and sang like the others, and called for the dancing women with the rest of them. If I had not been drunk, I might have observed that Absalom, sitting at the head of the table, was drinking very little, and now and then casting a dark and vengeful glance at me.

Suddenly I saw Absalom rise to his feet; and, pointing to me, he shouted to the assassins, who, unknown to me, were standing back of me, "There is the filthy wretch. Smite Amnon!" The words were hardly out of his mouth when I felt two swords pass through me like a flame of fire, and I fell from my seat to the floor. All the other sons of the king arose and fled. All the servants fled. All the dancing women fled. Absalom was gone. There I lay on the floor of the banqueting hall, my heart's blood pouring out. I was all alone, deserted by all.

It was Absalom who slew me, yet I deserved to die for my wicked crime against his sister. It was not Absalom's sword which slew me, but the sword of the Lord. Had I refrained from drink, I might not have committed that shameful, evil deed against Tamar. Or, had I refrained from drink the night of the banquet, I would have been on my guard and would not have been slain by Absalom. Let my death warn all of you. Beware of strong drink! It stirs up the appetites of the body; it unchains the demons of lust within the soul and brings men to shame, to death, and to darkness!

SOLOMON

Your royal robes, sir, betoken another king. This makes two kings, and the son of another king, who were drunkards.

Yes, I am Solomon, the wisest of kings, and yet the greatest of fools. I am the king who, when he came to the throne and knelt at Gibeon's holy altar, and, asked to choose what he would have, chose wisdom to rule and judge God's people. Because I did not ask for long life, or riches, or the life of my enemies, but only for wisdom, God made me wiser than all others, and richer than any king. He said to me that if I would walk in his ways, he would lengthen my days. What he promised, he gave. He gave me riches until gold became as brass, and silver as stones. He gave me wisdom that brought the queen of Sheba from afar to wonder at my knowledge. I wrote three thousand proverbs, and one thousand songs, and knew all nature, from the cedar of Lebanon to the hyssop that springeth out of the wall.

Yet I, the greatest and richest of kings, and, according to the standard of the world, the wisest of kings, was also the greatest of fools. Behold me now; not Solomon in all his glory, but Solomon in all his shame, grinding the face of the poor, seeking to slay my ministers, building altars to Baal and Molech for my seven hundred wives and three hundred concubines, who turned my heart away from God. Who would have thought that the young and eager king who once bowed at Gibeon and asked for wisdom to judge God's people, the king who built the Temple and dedicated it with prayer, is the same king who bent his aged knees at the altars of heathen gods? In all the Bible was there a fall like mine? The Arabs of the desert, to this day, tell of a worm that was eating out the heart of the staff upon which Solomon leaned. Although great was my fall, I am now wise enough by experience to say to you that your fame, your wisdom, your riches, are all in vain if you try to live without God. Listen! Can you hear the gnawing of that worm?

I am Solomon, the greatest of kings, and once the wisest, but I fell, and great was the fall thereof. My father, David, who gave me the throne, also fell, but who could think of David, even in his darkest days, doing what I did —bending his knees at the altars of heathen gods?

No words of warning as to the woe and curse of strong drink are more quoted in the pulpits of your churches, in public meetings, and in the press, than those words of mine which you will find in my book of Proverbs. Do not imagine that this is just rhetoric on my part, or second-hand warnings based on the experience of others. Alas, no! They are based on my own experience.

Turn, if you will, to my book of Ecclesiastes. There you will learn how I made great experiment to get at the heart of life and discover its true meaning. I tried wisdom, but found it a weariness of the flesh. I tried authorship, and found that in making of books there is no end. I tried architecture, and built the house in the wood, where the three hundred shields of gold hung on the wall, and where golden lions guarded my ivory throne. I tried engineering, and built fountains and pools and reservoirs for the good of the people. I tried agriculture, and set out gardens and orchards and trees. I tried husbandry, and had cattle on a thousand hills. I tried music and entertainment, and songs, and women, and dances. I tried silver and gold, and all the treasures of kings; but all this I found to be vanity and vanity of vanities.

Then I tried one thing more. I said to my soul, I will

try one more experiment. I will prove myself with mirth. I will give myself unto wine. Hence, the next time you hear spoken or read, or read for yourself, these words of mine on strong drink, remember, the man who wrote them knows they are true:

Wine is a mocker, strong drink is raging: and whosoever is deceived thereby is not wise. . . . Who hath woe? who hath contentions? who hath babbling? who hath wounds without cause? who hath redness of eyes? They that tarry long at the wine; they that go to seek mixed wine. Look not thou upon the wine when it is red, when it giveth his colour in the cup, when it moveth itself aright. At the last it biteth like a serpent, and stingeth like an adder.

VII

THE MOTHER OF RUFUS

A Salute to Mothers

> "Salute Rufus chosen in the Lord, and
> his mother and mine."
>
> Rom. 16:13

THE LAST CHAPTER OF THE LETTER TO THE ROMANS IS
one of my favorite chapters in the Bible. "Why," you say,
"that is strange. It is just a collection of names!" Yes;
and that is the very reason I like it. Because it is a collection of names, it is the most personal book in the Bible.
These twenty-six names were all personalities. Each one
had his joy and sorrow, his burden of care, his hope and
disappointment, his trial and tribulation. They all drank of
the cup of human experience; and, what is more important,
they all in some way had come to know Christ as their
Friend and Saviour.

I like to muse over these twenty-six names, about most
of whom we know nothing: Priscilla and Aquila, who in
some great trial and danger that befell the Apostle had,
he says, "for my life laid down their own necks"; and
Mary, "who bestowed much labour on us"; Andronicus
and Junia, "my kinsmen, . . . who also were in Christ before me." And there was Urbane. We wonder if his, or
her, character was urbane, like the name? And there was

Apelles, "approved in Christ"; and Herodion, another relative of Paul; and the family of Narcissus, "which are in the Lord"; and Julia and Olympas; and all these others with their beautiful Greek and Latin names. As each one is named, we wonder what he or she was like. Where had they fallen in with Paul? Were some of them of the number who later on, when Paul was coming a prisoner to Rome, went out fifty miles from Rome to Appii Forum and to the Three Taverns, and cheered and strengthened his heart with their welcome?

Sometimes you hear the cheap and shallow saying, "Christianity has never been tried." I scorn, deny, repudiate, and reject that saying! I say it has been tried, tried beautifully, gloriously, triumphantly, in the lives of those who before this evil world confessed the name of Christ. Paul knew some of them, and spoke of them as those "whose names are in the book of life." Here he sends his greetings and salutations to these twenty-six disciples at Rome who had nobly tried Christianity. Every age has produced them; and you and I know some of a more recent date, and near to us, who tried Christianity and succeeded. Some of them have their names written in the pages of the family Bible, between the Old Testament and the New Testament; and their names are written, too, in the Lamb's Book of Life. You are not ashamed of them! Christ is not ashamed of them, and they shall walk with him in white.

When we come to tell the story of great men, we like to commence with their ancestors. Luke in his Gospel says of John the Baptist that his father and mother,

Zacharias and Elisabeth, were "both righteous before God." But when we come to the story of Paul, we suffer a certain handicap, for we know little or nothing about Paul's ancestors. All that he tells us is that he was of pure Hebrew descent, a Hebrew of the Hebrews, and of the tribe of Benjamin, and that his father was a Pharisee. Luke mentions also a nephew of Paul, who revealed to the captain of the guard at Jerusalem the plot to assassinate the Apostle. Then in this Letter to the Romans, Paul mentions six persons at Rome who were his relatives. But there is no mention of his mother, the one about whom, above all others, we should like to know.

Standing once by one of the great turning water wheels in Tarsus, where Paul was born, and near which little children were playing, I wondered if Paul as a child played with other children at that same spot. And did he live on that very street? And what of his mother? When they told her that she had given birth to a man child, did her heart leap with the hope that perhaps this might be the long-promised Messiah? Did she stand on the dock at the port of Tarsus and wave a farewell to her son as he set off on the ship for Jerusalem to take a graduate course and sit at the feet of the great Gamaliel? Did she hear with maternal pride of his advancement in his studies? Of the prominent place that he was taking and of the part he was playing in the persecution of the odious sect of the Nazarenes and Christians? Did a sword of anguish pierce her heart when one day the word came to Tarsus and to the parents of Paul that their brilliant son had apostatized from the faith of Moses and had become a Christian? To all this we have no answer, save that of imagination.

However, in this chapter of greetings to the Christians at Rome we come upon this salutation, "Salute Rufus chosen in the Lord, and his mother and mine." There are two possibilities here: first, that Paul means two mothers, the mother of Rufus and his own.[1] Perhaps during his long stay at Tarsus after his conversion, and before he was called by Barnabas to take up the work at Antioch, Paul won his household, his father and mother and the rest of the family, to Christ; and perhaps his mother had found her way to Rome with these six other relatives and kinsmen whom Paul mentions. This is a possibility.

The other interpretation is that when he says, "Salute Rufus . . . , and his mother and mine," he is sending a greeting to Rufus' mother, who had also at some time played the part of a kind mother to him. If so, we wonder where and when it was. Was it in Asia or in Europe? Was it when he was sick? Did she nurse him back to health? Did she perhaps weave that robe and cloak that Paul left behind him in the house of Carpus at Troas? Did she make his thorn in the flesh more tolerable? Was she one of that band that went out to meet him at the Three Taverns when he was a prisoner to Rome? Did she afterward visit him in the Mamertine dungeon? Mark, who had association with Paul, and whose Gospel has always been associated with Rome, tells us that Simon of Cyrene, who carried the cross for Jesus to Calvary, was the father of

---

[1] The fact that Paul salutes a number of relatives in Rome suggests that possibly his own mother was there.

Alexander and Rufus. Perhaps this is the very Rufus whom Paul salutes; and if so, then the mother of Rufus was the wife of that Simon who is immortal because he bore the cross of Jesus.

But however all this may have been, and however interesting these conjectures, and whether by "his mother and mine" Paul means just the mother of Rufus, who had done the kindly office of a mother to him, or his own mother also, we take the beautiful greeting as a text for Mother's Day, and we salute all mothers with these words of the Apostle. There are those who say that Mother's Day is a lot of sentiment. It is, indeed; but it is good sentiment. It is the kind of sentiment that can wipe some of the dust and stain of the world from our eyes and from our souls. Not all mothers, unfortunately, are, in character, worthy of salutation. But, in office, in the sacred relationship of motherhood, they are worthy of salutation.

A MOTHER AND SACRIFICIAL LOVE

Why do we salute good mothers? Because a good mother is the symbol and incarnation of sacrificial love and care. In the Lithuanian speech the word for mother means "martyr." And how appropriate that is! Psalm 103 says that "like as a father pitieth his children, so the Lord pitieth them that fear him." But when the Bible comes to speak of the utmost of human love, it finds the gauge and standard of it, not in a father's love, but in a mother's, for it asks, "Can a woman forget her sucking child?"

A picture of beautiful sacrificial motherhood is that of

Rizpah, one of the wives of King Saul. When her two sons had been hung up before the Lord by David as a satisfaction to the Gibeonites, because Saul had disregarded the covenant made with them long before by Joshua, and had sacked their towns and had slain their people, she took her stand where the bodies of her sons were hanging, exposed to the weather and to the vultures and the beasts. There she spread her sackcloth on a great rock for a tent and took up her sad and lonely vigil, a vigil which lasted from the beginning of the barley harvest until the first rain came at the end of the summer. By day and by night there she stood, defending the bodies of her sons. By day her waving cudgel drove off the circling birds and vultures, and by night her waving torch drove off the prowling jackal and wolf.

David could be cruel at times, but he was also magnanimous; and when he heard of this mother's devotion, he went in person to Gibeon, took down the bodies of Rizpah's two sons and the five others who had been hanged with them, and gave them decent and honorable sepulture in the tomb of Saul's father, Kish, in the land of Benjamin. In the long annals of sacrificial motherhood we know of nothing more beautiful or moving than Rizpah's devotion. I would like to be an artist and paint that picture! Only a mother could have done it! Her noble act is a picture, or symbol, of a mother's care for the bodies of her children, and, still more, for the welfare of their souls.

A mother is a man's best and safest sweetheart. The British poet, Thomas Campbell, author of the famous poems "Hohenlinden," "The Soldier's Dream," and "The

Pleasures of Hope," wrote an interesting poem on "Napoleon and the British Sailor." It is based upon a historic incident. It was the time when Napoleon had gathered his army and his ships at Boulogne and was threatening to invade England, just as Hitler threatened to do after the fall of Dunkirk. The French navy had captured a British sailor, but for some reason they did not imprison him, but permitted him "unprisoned on the shore to roam." Always this British seaman was gazing wistfully toward the white cliffs of Dover, beyond which lay his home. One morning, as he walked along the seashore, he saw an empty hogshead come floating shoreward. He pulled the hogshead up on the shore and hid it in a cave. There every day he toiled at his work of turning the hogshead into a boat. At length he had fashioned a rude boat and bound it together with wattled willows, and with this frail craft "untarred, uncompassed, and unkeeled," and with no sail or rudder, he was going to paddle his way across the stormy channel to his homeland. But just as he was setting out on his journey, the Frenchmen discovered him and brought him back to the shore, where they laughed and jeered at his little cockle of a boat, his "little Argo." Napoleon heard of this venture, and, always ready to recognize heroism in soldiers and sailors, he summoned this British sailor before him and said to him:

> "Rash man, that wouldst yon Channel pass
>   On twigs and staves so rudely fashioned,
> Thy heart with some sweet British lass
>   Must be impassioned."

"I have no sweetheart," said the lad;
 "But—absent long from one another—
Great was the longing that I had
 To see my mother."

Greatly moved at this,
          "And so thou shalt," Napoleon said,
          "Ye've both my favor fairly won."

So saying, he gave the British tar a piece of gold and
sent him off with a flag of truce to England and to his
mother. Yes! The best and safest sweetheart that a man
has is always a good mother.

A MOTHER AND PURITY

Another reason we salute our mothers is that a good
mother is the symbol of purity and honor in life. In his
essay on Jean Paul Richter, Carlyle quotes a fine sentence
of Richter, that "every man who has had a good mother
regards all women as sacred for her sake." I wish that
this were so. The thought of a good mother has often
kept a man from doing evil. In Philadelphia I once went
to see a young man in prison. He had fallen into temptation and stolen property. He came from a good home in
the South. I remember the first thing he said to me was,
"Don't tell my mother!" He could not bear the thought of
his Christian mother, who had loved and prayed for him,
learning that he was a thief.

On one occasion a group of Civil War officers were
celebrating a reunion. Each one in turn arose and made a
speech or told a story or made some other contribution

to the evening's entertainment. As the wine flowed more freely, the stories and jests became more salacious and indecent. At length it came the turn of an officer who had been rather quiet and aloof during the evening's jollification. Rising to his feet when his turn came, he filled his glass and, holding it aloft, said, "I propose a toast, Our mothers!" At once a hush fell over the ribald group. What had happened? Each one had seen the face of his mother.

A MOTHER AND FAITH IN GOD

Faith is something that can be passed on. Paul knew this when he reminded Timothy of the "unfeigned faith" that had dwelt in his mother Eunice and his grandmother Lois, "and I am persuaded in thee also." Lois, that godly grandmother, passed her faith on to Eunice, and Eunice passed it on to Timothy. Henry Ward Beecher, when he was troubled by doubts, as most men at one time or another in their life are, and who often paid beautiful tribute to that great mother Roxanna Foote, said:

Now you may put all the skeptical men that ever lived on the face of the earth on one side, and they may plead in my ears, and all the scientists may stand with them and marshal all the facts in the universe to disprove the truth of Immanuel—God with us. And yet let me see my mother walking in a great sorrow, but reflecting the light of cheer and heavenly hope, sweet, patient, gentle, full of comfort for others, and that single instance of suffering is more to me as an evidence of the truth of Christianity than all the arguments that the wisest men can possibly bring against it.

Of all mothers I would like to ask this question: By what would you like your son or daughter to remember you? A woman in great agony and distress, who had suffered as cruel a blow as any woman can, said to me at the end of her sorrowful recital, "Oh, if it had not been for my mother's Bible—" She did not finish the sentence, and there was no need for her to do so. In the storm and darkness that had come down over her life, her mother's Bible reminded her of her mother's faith and her mother's God. Now that recollection was an anchor for her soul.

And to you who are sons and daughters, I would like to say this, How near or far are you from what your mother desired you to be? There is an old hymn that used to be sung, and was often irreverently mocked and parodied, "Tell Mother I'll Be There." But I shall never forget the night I sat in the gallery of a great auditorium in the West and joined with thousands of others in singing, at the end of a stirring evangelistic sermon, the lines of that hymn. Then it was nothing to ridicule or mock, but thousands of souls sending up a message to mothers in heaven.

There is an old and beautiful tradition that the angel who let Peter out of the prison of Herod was his own departed mother. Just a legend; but it embodies the truth that the memory of a good mother often takes a man by the hand and leads him out of the bondage and darkness of unbelief and sin into the light of truth and salvation.

VIII

NAOMI

A Great Mother-in-Law

"Call me not Naomi."   Ruth 1 :20

In spite of your request, we shall insist upon calling you Naomi, which means "Pleasantness," for of all the women in the Bible we know of no one who better deserves this title. All thy ways are pleasantness, and all thy paths are peace.

To my mind, Naomi is almost the most beautiful name in the Bible. Sometimes we see a person with a beautiful name whose personality does not harmonize with the name. In the vivid metaphor of Proverbs, the name is like a jewel in a swine's snout. But here there is complete agreement between the name and the personality of the woman who bore it. In the book of Ruth we have two great women, the mother-in-law and the daughter-in-law; and sometimes I fear that in praising the great daughter-in-law and the beauty of her character, we overlook the great mother-in-law, the beauty of her character, and the place she took in the unfolding of God's plan for the redemption of the world.

The four-chapter book of Ruth is so small that sometimes you can hardly find it when you search through the books of the Old Testament, where it comes between the book of Judges and the first book of Samuel. The book of Judges is full of violence, assassination, and other crimes, together, of course, with the record of noble men and noble women. The book of Samuel begins to a beautiful note with the birth of Samuel. But many of its pages deal with the decline and fall of King Saul, and his jealous rage and fierce pursuit of David, and his tragic death in battle with the Philistines on Mount Gilboa. But in between these two books of violence comes this lovely pastoral idyll, like a sweet interlude in a tremendous chorus of violence and war. In these pages there does not appear a single evil-minded person. There is no act of violence, no crime, no cry of the dying upon a battlefield, no sacked and smoking cities, no fierce vengeance. It is a book of peace. In this respect, because it gives us a link in the chain in the descent and ancestry of Jesus, it is a fitting prelude to the birth of another Child at this same Bethlehem long after.

Yet, although there is no war or violence or bloodshed in this book, there is, as there must be in every book of life, sorrow and trial, and death's inevitable shadow. Yet with sorrow and death and trial there is wonderful love and devotion.

AFFLICTION IN A STRANGE LAND

It was during the iron age of the judges, when there was no king in Israel, and every man did that which was right in his own eyes. In Bethlehem, where Jesus was born centuries afterward, there lived a man whose name was Elimelech. He fell in love with a young and beautiful woman of Bethlehem, who bore the name of Naomi. After their marriage two sons were born to them— Mahlon and Chilion. At first all went well with the family; but there came a time when the rainfall was scanty, and as a result the harvest was poor. There was a famine in the land. Word came to Elimelech that eastward in Moab, across the Jordan, there was bread. Moab was a heathen land and was under the judgment of God for its inhospitality to the children of Israel on their march toward the land of Canaan. But men must have bread. Elimelech put aside racial prejudice and migrated with his family eastward into Moab. The villagers at Bethlehem gathered about them and bade the family farewell, as with high hopes they started for the new country.

At first things prospered with them in the land of Moab; but they had not been there long when Elimelech died, leaving Naomi, the young widow, with her two sons, Mahlon and Chilion. In the course of time, Mahlon married a daughter of Moab called Ruth; and the other son, Chilion, married a young woman called Orpah. They had not been married long when first Mahlon died, and then Chilion. Thus Naomi in a short time was bereft not only of her husband, but also of her two sons. The two daughters-in-law, Ruth and Orpah, continued to live with their widowed mother-in-law.

RUTH'S AVOWAL

Sorrow turns the heart homeward. As long as Elimelech lived, and after his death, as long as Mahlon and Chilion lived, Naomi felt that she could continue to dwell in the strange land of Moab. But now, when her multiplied sorrows came upon her, her heart turned to what the Scottish folk call "my ain countrie." If Naomi had to meet loneliness and sorrow, she felt she could better do it among her own people. She said to herself, as Hadad, whom Solomon had driven into Egypt, said when Pharaoh pressed him to stay, "Let me depart, that I may go to mine own country."

When Naomi announced her intention to return to Bethlehem, her two daughters said that they would go with her, in spite of Naomi's unselfish advice that it would be better for them to remain in their own country and let her go home alone. They journeyed with her for some distance, probably as far as the borderline between Moab and Canaan. There Naomi again told them to return, each one to her mother's house, and made the prayer that the Lord would deal kindly with them, as they had dealt with the dead and with Naomi. When she kissed them good-bye, still weeping, Ruth and Orpah clung to her, and said, "Surely we will return with thee unto thy people." But Naomi again urged them to go back to their own home. There they would be much more likely, she told them, to find husbands among their own people than in a strange land. It grieved her much, she said, that they were involved in her own afflictions; and, as far as possible, she wanted to lift this shadow and handicap from them.

In answer to this new appeal, Orpah kissed her mother-in-law and bade her farewell. But Ruth "clave unto her." Once more Naomi pleaded with Ruth to go back with her sister-in-law. "Behold, thy sister in law is gone back to her people, and unto her gods: return thou after thy sister in law." But Ruth said—and in all the Bible nothing was more earnestly or more beautifully said—"Intreat me not to leave thee, or to return from following after thee: for whither thou goest, I will go; and where thou lodgest, I will lodge: thy people shall be my people, and thy God my God: where thou diest, will I die, and there will I be buried: the Lord do so to me, and more also, if ought but death part thee and me." Where soul is joined with soul and heart with heart, no nobler utterance was ever made.

When she heard these words of devotion and decision from her daughter-in-law, Naomi no longer remonstrated with her. Together they set out for Bethlehem. At length Naomi saw in the distance the familiar features of the little town, with the hills about it. Although she had not been there for years now, everything was familiar, for the towns of the East changed slowly then, and just about as slowly now. Deep emotions now stirred within the heart of Naomi as she saw her childhood home and thought of the simple joys and the ardent dreams of her girlhood; her courtship by the young man Elimelech; her marriage; the first child, Mahlon, who was born to her; and then Chilion; the coming of hard times, and the day of their departure to the land of Moab.

A ROMANCE OF THE HARVEST

As soon as the word spread that Naomi was coming home, all the villagers turned out to greet her, for she had been well known and well loved in the town. They remembered Naomi as a pretty girl, a lovely bride, a handsome young mother. But now, as they gathered about her and saw upon her face the marks of time and bereavement, they could hardly believe that it was she, and said one to another, "Is this Naomi?" Naomi answered for herself. "Yes, this is Naomi, the same Naomi you used to know, and yet not the same. Call me not Naomi, call me Mara: for the Almighty hath dealt very bitterly with me. I went out full, and the Lord hath brought me home again empty: why then call ye me Naomi, seeing the Lord hath testified against me, and the Almighty hath afflicted me?"

It was the barley harvest when Naomi and her daughter-in-law reached Bethlehem. After the affectionate greetings of the people were over, the two widows, the young widow and the old widow, had to meet the problem of existence. They must have bread. The courageous Ruth said to her mother, "Let me now go to the field, and glean ears of corn after him in whose sight I shall find grace." And she said unto her, "Go, my daughter."

Ruth knew not what field it was she was going into where she saw the reapers at work; but "her hap was to light on a part of the field belonging unto Boaz," a well-to-do and honorable man. As we shall see, this apparent chance played a very important part in the history of Naomi and Ruth; and, in the course of time, in the destiny of mankind.

The harvest field in the Near East, to this very day, is a stirring and picturesque sight. The men and women with their sickles, and the grain falling before the sweep of the sharp knives. The women clad in their bright garments, chiefly yellow and blue and red. On the threshing floor the grain being thrown up into the air with the wind carrying the chaff away. "Like the chaff which the wind driveth away."

Ruth spoke to the foreman of the field, and asked if she might be permitted to glean after the reapers. This was a privilege which was always granted to a stranger and the foreigner and the needy. Through the law of ancient Israel there ran a crimson thread of mercy and compassion. It was commanded that when they reaped the fields they were not to reap wholly the corners of the field, but leave something for the stranger; and when they beat the trees for their fruit, they were not to strip them completely, but leave something for the stranger. Ruth, as a stranger, was permitted by this custom to glean after the reapers.

By and by the landlord, Boaz, came into the field to see how things were going. He was at once attracted by the beautiful stranger in the field, and inquired of his foreman who she was. When he learned that it was the Moabitish damsel who had come back to Bethlehem with her mother-in-law, Naomi, Boaz went over to her and spoke kindly to her, telling her to remain always near to his maidens when she was working in the field. Ruth, with great courtesy, thanked her benefactor and asked him how it was that she had found grace in his eyes, seeing she was a stranger. Boaz answered that he had learned of her kindness to her mother-in-law, and how she had left her own father and mother and come as a stranger into the new country. He then made the heartfelt prayer, for he was a godly man, that she would have a full reward from the God of Israel, "under whose wings thou art come to trust."

At the noontide hour, when the reapers sat down to eat and drink, Boaz saw that a goodly portion was given to Ruth; and when she went out into the field to glean in the afternoon, he told the young men to let "fall also some of the handfuls of purpose" for her, that she might glean them, and rebuke her not. "Handfuls of purpose!" What a quaint, beautiful phrase this is, and what a pity to have it spoiled and changed by any new or revised edition of the Bible! Boaz did not want Ruth to feel embarrassed by the reapers' openly leaving ungleaned an unusual portion of the field, but asked them to do it quietly, unobservedly, and yet generously. The result was that when Ruth got home that night, she carried in her veil an ephah of barley. Her mother-in-law said to her, "Where hast thou gleaned today? . . . Blessed be he that did take knowledge of thee." When Ruth told her the name of the man who owned the field, Naomi remembered that Boaz was a kinsman of her dead husband. "Blessed be he of the Lord, who hath not left off his kindness to the living and to the dead."

Every day after that, Ruth went out to the field of Boaz to glean after the reapers, and returned every evening with a generous portion of grain. At length these visits resulted, as one might have expected, in marriage; but not without some wise and shrewd assistance on the part of Naomi. When their child was born, Naomi took the child and laid it in her bosom and became a nurse unto it. They called his name Obed. Obed became the father of Jesse, and Jesse was the father of David; and of David's line another Babe was born at Bethlehem ages afterward whose name was Jesus.

NAOMI AND DESTINY

The book of Ruth closes in a fitting way, with Naomi as the chief personality, for it is to her that the women of the town speak. They tell Naomi that the child which has been born unto her daughter-in-law shall be unto her a restorer of her life and a nourisher of her old age, and that his name shall be famous in Israel—more famous, indeed, than any one of them at that time could know.

When we look at Naomi, we behold a woman altogether unselfish. Her husband was dead; her sons were dead. But she gave her love to her daughters-in-law. Selfless love is the unmistakable trait of true motherhood. Naomi was unwilling that the grief which had fallen upon her should shadow the life of Ruth. This self-denial and sacrifice came back to her with interest a hundredfold.

It must not be forgotten that when Ruth made her beautiful avowal and said to Naomi, "Thy people shall be my people, and thy God my God," it was the choice and decision of a woman who had been an idolater choosing now the only true God. There is no record that during their life together in Moab, Naomi had given her daughter-in-law instruction as to the true faith. Nevertheless, she won Ruth to the God of Israel by the silent and powerful eloquence of her character and her life. There is no stronger Godward influence than that of a godly mother.

After an infidel had been plying a man with arguments against Christianity and the existence of a God, he said to him, thinking that he had demolished all his defenses, "What have you left now?" The man answered, "My mother's life." He knew that such a life was an infallible witness to the existence of a God. It was the life of this mother-in-law which commended her God and her religion to her daughter-in-law. Does your character, your life, commend your God to others? Would it lead anyone to say, "Thy God shall be my God, and thy people shall be my people"?

All through this book of Ruth runs the scarlet cord of providence and destiny. The death of Naomi's husband, the migration to Moab, the death of her two sons, the return to Bethlehem, her daughter-in-law going out into the field to glean after the reapers, and that field happening to be the field of a kinsman; the meeting of Ruth and Boaz in the harvest field, and Naomi's wise suggestion to Ruth when she made her midnight venture to the threshing floor —all these were working out the plan of God and the coming of a Saviour. Both Ruth and Naomi, although unconsciously, were the agents of divine destiny.

When Naomi takes Ruth's child into her bosom, we see Mary, ages afterward, at the same Bethlehem, taking the child Jesus into her bosom. Every mother and every father, and every brother and every sister, and every son and every daughter, who lives honorably and kindly and unselfishly, like Naomi, with faith in God, becomes thereby a co-worker with God, and carries forward his wise and beautiful plan for the redemption of mankind.

IX

AGRIPPA

The Almost Christian

> "I would to God, that not only thou, but
> also all that hear me this day, were both
> almost, and altogether such as I am,
> except these bonds."
>
> Acts 26:29

YOU MIGHT BE ABLE TO SAY TO ANOTHER, "I WISH THAT
you were as good a Christian as my godly mother." Or,
you might say, "I wish you were as good a Christian as
Peter, or John, or Barnabas, or Paul." But what about
yourself? How far could you go in wishing that another
man were a Christian like you, except for some external
handicap of body or worldly circumstance? Paul wished
that King Agrippa were not almost, but altogether, such
as he was, except his bonds, the chain with which he was
bound to a soldier. Could you and I say that?

Several years now Paul had been a prisoner at Caesarea,
whither he had been taken by the Roman officers at Jerusalem to save him from the fury of the mob which
sought to tear him to pieces, and from the conspiracy of
forty assassins who had taken a vow that they would
neither eat nor drink until they had killed Paul. The first
governor before whom his case was heard was Felix. After

the trial, in which Paul was accused of sedition and treason, and against which he eloquently defended himself, Felix reserved judgment. But his interest in this singular prisoner was such that he invited him to preach before him and his mistress, Drusilla. The sermon was a great surprise to Felix and his paramour. Instead of hearing something about Jewish laws or customs, Felix heard a sermon on righteousness and temperance and judgment to come. The sermon made him tremble. But, instead of repenting and believing, Felix said, "When I have a convenient season, I will call for thee." He did have what he thought was a convenient season, and frequently called for Paul to preach to him. But never again did Paul make Felix tremble. His opportunity had passed. For three years Felix kept Paul in prison, hoping that some of his friends would offer him a bribe for his release.

Felix was succeeded as governor of Judea by Porcius Festus. The Jews tried to get Festus to send Paul up to Jerusalem to be tried, planning to assassinate him on the way. But Paul, knowing that his life would be in jeopardy, refused to go. Instead, he availed himself of his privilege and right as a Roman citizen and made his appeal to the supreme court of the Empire: "I stand at Caesar's judgment seat. . . . I appeal unto Caesar." Recognizing the Apostle's right of appeal, Festus gave it his official sanction, saying, "Unto Caesar thou shalt go."

While Festus was waiting for a convenient ship on which to send Paul to Rome, King Agrippa and his sister, Bernice, also the sister of Drusilla, the mistress of Felix, came to pay Festus a visit. Agrippa, an apostate

Jew, was the great-grandson of Herod the Great. Festus mentioned to Agrippa the case of his prisoner Paul, and how he had been surprised to learn that it had nothing to do—as he had supposed—with wicked and lawless acts, but seemed to be a dispute about points of Jewish law, and about a man named Jesus, whom the Jews said was dead, but whom Paul declared to be alive. Agrippa said that he would like to hear Paul himself. To this Festus gladly agreed, and on the next day Paul was summoned before them.

The palace hall of the Roman governor at Caesarea displayed, no doubt, all the features of official Roman architecture at that time. Its walls were high and massive, the floor was of marble and tile, and the roof was upheld by stately columns. Along the walls were hung the insignia of the Roman Empire. Here and there appeared the ancient imperial sign, SPQR, the People and the Senate of Rome; and here and there also appeared in purple the large letter "N," standing for the emperor, Nero. Ranged along the walls stood the Roman soldiers belonging to the crack regiment, or legion, the Italian Band, then stationed at Caesarea. Their high, eagle-crowned helmets flashed in the bright light, and the short sword was girt on their thigh. The veterans had a look of contempt and scorn in their face, and wondered why there was much ado about a despised Hebrew prisoner.

Presently there was the sound of a trumpet. The curtains behind the dais were drawn aside, and Festus conducted Agrippa and Bernice to their chairs of state. Immediately the soldiers stretched out their right hands in

114

the salute which was again made familiar to the world by the followers of Mussolini and Hitler. When Festus and Bernice and Agrippa had taken their seats, there was another blast on the trumpet, and the prisoner was brought in. With the hand that was not chained to the soldier next to him, Paul shaded his weak eyes from the glare of the light. He was conducted to a place in front of the throne and there waited in silence until Festus spoke. Festus gave Agrippa another brief account of Paul and the charges against him, saying that he was somewhat perplexed as to what information he should send along to Caesar when Paul was taken to Rome, and expressed the hope that Agrippa would help him in this matter. Then Agrippa said to Paul, "Thou art permitted to speak for thyself."

PAUL'S APPEAL

With his familiar gesture, Paul stretched forth his hand and began to speak. He first expressed his pleasure at being able to plead his case before one who was so familiar with Jewish history and customs. Then followed the story of his devout youth, his persecution of Christ and the Church, his dramatic conversion at Damascus, and how he was commissioned to go unto the Gentiles, to open their eyes and turn them from darkness to light and from the power of Satan unto God, that they might receive forgiveness of sins, and inheritance among those who are sanctified by faith.

As he waxed eloquent and earnest in his account of how Christ had suffered and risen again, that he might give salvation to the world, he was suddenly interrupted, not by Agrippa, but by Festus, who said, "Paul, thou art beside thyself; much learning doth make thee mad!" It was when Paul reached the Resurrection in his sermon on Mars Hill that the philosophers mocked and broke up the meeting. Now Festus thought that Paul was crazy, because he talked about a man who had been raised from the dead. "Much learning doth make thee mad!"

With admirable self-control, Paul made an earnest disavowal of mental aberration, saying, "I am not mad, most noble Festus; but speak forth the words of truth and soberness." It would not be a bad thing for the Church today if its preachers were so earnest and so true to the gospel that the charge of madness would be brought against them. Paul was not mad, but in dead earnest, burning with the fervor of tremendous conviction. He told Festus that he had sopken words that were true, things that the king himself knew about. Then he turned dramatically to King Agrippa on the throne, exclaiming, "King Agrippa, believest thou the prophets?" Then, before Agrippa had time to reply, he added, "I know that thou believest." And that, no doubt, was true. Apostate Jew though he was, Agrippa had great respect for the prophets of Israel, and it was plain from his attitude and the look on his face that he was convinced that Paul was correctly interpreting the prophets. Paul appealed, as all the early preachers of the gospel did, not only to the acts and events in the life of Jesus, which were well attested by witnesses, but also to the predictions of those events by the prophets. The prophecies and Christ stand or fall together; for, as Peter said when he preached to the centurion Cornelius, "To him give all the prophets witness."

When Paul made this direct appeal to Agrippa, and said, "I know that thou believest," Agrippa called out, "Almost thou persuadest me to be a Christian." If you and I had been there, and heard the accent of King Agrippa, and seen the look on his face, we should have known without doubt just what he meant. Was he, as is generally supposed, speaking in irony and sarcasm? As if to say: "Paul, do you think that with a little persuasion, with one sermon like this, you can make me a follower of your crucified Jesus? Do you think that a great-grandson of Herod the Great is going to take up with fishermen and peasants and slaves?" Was that the way Agrippa meant it? Was it just a derisive jest? Or did he say it in earnestness and sincerity? Was his conscience stirred within him? Had Paul touched the chords of his better nature? Was that why he cried out, "Almost thou persuadest me to be a Christian"? This, at least, was the way Paul took it; for immediately he responded—and here you see Paul in one of his grandest moments—"I would to God, that not only thou, but also all that hear me this day, were both almost, and altogether such as I am, except these bonds."

EXCEPT THESE BONDS

Before we take up the response that Agrippa made to this appeal, let us look at the nobility and grandeur of the wish that Paul expressed. He said his earnest desire was that Agrippa might be as he was, "except these bonds."

It was as if Paul had said, "I would that thou wert not almost, but altogether a believer in Jesus such as I am; all except this chain. I would not wish you to spend the years that I have spent in dark prisons. I would not wish for you my long and weary journeys over blazing plains and through wild gorges and over snow-covered mountains. I would not wish for you my terrible experiences in three shipwrecks. I would not wish for you the pain and agony of being stoned, as I was at Lystra, when I was dragged out of the gate of the city and left for dead. I would not wish for you the pain of being thrice beaten with rods by Roman soldiers, and five times with thirty-nine stripes by the Jews. I would not want you to be in perils of waters, in perils of robbers, in perils by your own countrymen, in perils in the city, in perils in the wilderness, in perils in the sea, in perils among false brethren, in weariness and painfulness, in watchings often, in hunger and thirst, in fastings often, in cold and nakedness. No; I would not wish that for you. But, King Agrippa, I would to God that you had my peace of soul; that you knew what it means to have Christ with you in the brightest hour and in the darkest hour of life. I wish that you could say, as I can say, 'For me to live is Christ, and to die is gain. To be with Christ is far better.' All this, Agrippa, I would to God that you knew and experienced. And not only you, King Agrippa, but you, too, most noble Festus, and you, too, most gracious Bernice; and all you lords and ladies here today; and you, the centurion, and all the soldiers and all that hear me this day, I would to God that all of you were as I am in Christ, except these chains. For his sake I bear this chain.

But, Agrippa, if I had to choose between Christ with a chain, or no chain and no Christ, I would choose Christ and this chain; for this chain and all my sufferings are but a small price to pay for the love and companionship of my Saviour Jesus Christ and the hope that I have in him."

"Except these bonds." In wishing that Agrippa were as he was, the only thing that Paul had to except was his chain. How is it with you and me? If you ask someone to be a Christian as you are, what would you have to except? Would it be your bad temper? your churlish disposition? your tongue which likes to speak evil of another? your tainted imagination? your fear and worry for tomorrow, instead of casting all your cares upon God? How many things are there that you would have to except? Christ said that every believer must be a witness unto him. When we remember this, and think with shame and confusion of the many things that we would have to except, let us confess our sin and seek the mercy of a pardoning God.

AGRIPPA'S ANSWER

Agrippa had been expecting only a dissertation on Jewish law and custom. Instead of that, Paul preached to his soul, the soul of a licentious, wicked man. He rang the bell in the innermost chamber of Agrippa's heart. He struck the hidden and long-silent chord of Agrippa's moral nature. Paul eagerly saw that what he was saying was making an impact on the conscience of the king; and, pressing his advantage, this great hunter for souls cried out, "King

Agrippa, believest thou the prophets? I know that thou believest!" Then he made his great adventure for the soul of Agrippa, "Would to God that thou wert almost and altogether as I am, except these chains."

What held Agrippa back? It may have been his pride. How could a descendant of the great Herod confess himself a stained and guilty sinner and throw himself on the mercy of the crucified Galilean? How could he take his place in singing hymns with fishermen and peasants and slaves? The first and fundamental qualification for saving belief in Christ is humility. Or perhaps it was the love of this present world that made Agrippa draw back. He thought of his high post as a king under the Roman Empire; his revenues, his slaves, his chariots, his palaces and villas—how could he give all these up and become a follower of the lowly Nazarene? Again, it may have been, and probably was, the sinful life that Agrippa was leading that held him back. It was generally accepted that he was living in sin with Bernice. This probably was only one of many shameful and wicked associations. But the love of his sin held him back. There is nothing strange about that. It still happens today.

Agrippa suddenly broke up the hearing, and stopped Paul's sermon by rising up from his seat. As he walked out of the audience chamber with Festus and Bernice, Agrippa said to Festus: "This man doeth nothing worthy of death or of bonds. He might have been set at liberty, if he had not appealed unto Caesar." That was what Agrippa said. He commented on the eloquence and sincerity of the preacher. But that was not what Paul wanted to hear from him. What Paul wanted to hear was what every true preacher wants to hear—not complimentary remarks, but a change of heart, and a decision for Christ. He wants to hear that those who are already Christians are determined to be better Christians, so that they, too, can say, "Such as I am, except these chains." He wants to hear that those who are not yet Christians shall become not "almost" Christians, but "altogether" Christians.

There have been many men who were, as Jesus said to one of the scribes, "not far from the kingdom of God." Among these was the rich young ruler whom Jesus loved, and who asked, "What must I do to inherit eternal life?" But when Jesus told him what he must do, he was not able to pay the price. And Herod Antipas, whose conscience was stirred by John the Baptist; who brought John up frequently from the prison and heard him preach, and who "did many things, and heard him gladly," which means that he started on the right path, but in the end beheaded John and mocked at Jesus. And Felix, who trembled when he heard Paul preach, but did nothing about it. And Pilate, who, the moment his eye fell on Jesus, recognized him as a just and true man, and strove in every way to escape the guilt of crucifying him; but who, when he heard the mob shout, "Thou art not Caesar's friend," delivered him up to be crucified. And King Agrippa, who said, "Almost thou persuadest me to be a Christian," but went no further.

When you are crossing the ocean, you will see from the deck of your vessel, far off on the horizon, other ships which emerge for a little out of the fog or darkness into the path of light—the sunlight or the moonlight—and then disappear again into fog or darkness. So in the Bible there are these men who appear for a moment in the precious light of conviction, of earnest spiritual desire, and then disappear in the clouds of indecision or in the darkness of rejection of Christ.

The most impressive part of any service, for a preacher who has proclaimed the Word of the Lord, is when the last hymn has been sung, the benediction has been pronounced, the organ commences to roll, and the congregation starts down the aisle for the doors. What will the true preacher be thinking? He will be thinking things like this: How quickly will the impression made in some heart fade away? That chord which was struck in the soul of some man, and which had long been silent, when will it become silent again? How many of those who have listened to the sermon, and have said to themselves, "I would like to be a Christian—not almost, but altogether," are going to act on this divine impulse? And that one whose heart was stirred and whose conscience was awakened with sorrow for sin, will he go on to repentance, or will he turn back again to his sin?

Yes; the most solemn part of the service is when the service is over. I wonder what Paul thought, or what he said, if he said anything, to the soldier at his side as he led him back to his cell? He had done his best. He had brought a soul *almost* into the Kingdom, but not altogether. But almost is not enough; almost is but to fail.

122

Why not altogether? May the great Apostle's words echo not in vain in every soul here this day—"I would to God, that not only thou, but also all that hear me this day, were both almost, and altogether such as I am, except these bonds."

X

MALCHUS
The Last Miracle

"And he touched his ear, and healed
him."   Luke 22:51

THE LAST MIRACLE OF JESUS BEFORE HIS DEATH WAS,
in some respects, the most beautiful and touching of all.
It was a fitting and lovely climax to that long series of
gracious and healing miracles. His first miracle was
wrought at the marriage in Cana of Galilee. It was done
at an occasion of joy and mirth and happiness. This last
miracle was done in the shadows of Gethsemane, a time
and a place of sorrow and travail of soul and agony.
Against this dark background shines the beauty of Christ's
last miracle.

When Jesus worked his first miracle at Cana of Galilee
and turned water into wine, the astonished governor of
the feast, when he had tasted the wine, called the bride-
groom and said to him, "Every man at the beginning
doth set forth good wine; . . . then that which is worse:
but thou hast kept the good wine until now." So it might be
said concerning the miracles of Jesus. He kept the best
wine, the best miracle, until the last. It was a miracle done
when he was suffering. It was done not in response to a
cry for pity and help from some troubled soul, but in

124

answer to the blow of an enemy. Jesus said, "Love your enemies, bless them that curse you, do good to them that hate you, and pray for them which despitefully use you, and persecute you." This was his great text, and here in Gethsemane is his great illustration of the text. He practiced what he preached.

All four Gospels relate the fact that when Jesus was seized by his enemies in the Garden of Gethsemane, one of his disciples drew a sword and smote off the ear of the servant of the high priest. Only John gives us the name of that servant, Malchus, and only John gives us the name of the disciple who drew the sword, Peter. But even if the name had not been given, it would have been an easy guess that it was Peter who smote with the sword. Perhaps the authors of the other three Gospels, written earlier than John's, when many of the actors in the scenes of that last night were still alive, felt it would be a protection to Peter not to give his name, whereas John, writing much later, felt it would be safe then to give the name of Peter. Only Luke among the four Gospels gives us the account of this last miracle, how Jesus put forth his hand and touched the man's ear and healed him.

The Supper was over. The traitor had gone out into the night with Satan in his heart to betray Jesus. The farewell address had been spoken. The sublime intercessory prayer had been offered, and a closing hymn had been sung. Then Jesus led the eleven disciples down the road and across the bridge over the Brook Kedron, and up the other side into the Garden of Gethsemane, where he left eight of the disciples near the gate and, with Peter and James and John, went farther into the Garden. There, charging them to watch with him, he removed himself from them a stone's cast, and entered into his agony. Now he was coming out of that agony. Coming to the disciples for the third time, and finding them asleep again, he said, "Sleep on now, and take your rest." Then, in a moment he spoke another word, "Rise, let us be going: behold, he is at hand that doth betray me."

Presently the mob, led by Judas, their torches dancing in the night, pressed through the gate of the Garden seeking their prey. Facing the mob, Jesus said unto them, "Whom seek ye?" They answered, "Jesus of Nazareth." Jesus said unto them, "I am he." When they heard that, the mob recoiled and fell to the ground. For a moment the majesty of the Son of God overcame them. Then, recovering themselves, they gathered about Jesus to seize him. At that, Peter drew his sword, and aiming it at one whom he had seen strike Jesus, and who was the servant of the high priest, he smote off his ear. At once Jesus said to Peter: "Put up again thy sword into his place: for all they that take the sword shall perish with the sword. Thinkest thou that I cannot now pray to my Father, and he shall presently give me more than twelve legions of angels? . . . The cup which my father hath given me, shall I not drink it?" Then he stretched forth his hand and touched the ear of Malchus and healed him. So with this beautiful act of mercy and forgiveness the book of the miracles of Jesus comes to a close.

VIOLENCE AND THE GOSPEL OF CHRIST

Peter was loyal to his Master that night when he drew that sword, and you can hardly keep from cheering him when you see him strike that blow in defense of his Master. He was loyal, but he was mistaken. That night, before they had gone out into the Garden, Jesus had said, "He that hath no sword, let him sell his garment, and buy one." Peter understood Jesus in a literal sense; but evidently Jesus was speaking figuratively, meaning that the lives of all the disciples would be filled with difficulty and hardship, and everywhere they would confront the opposition of the world. The Koran promises sensual joys and pleasures in heaven for all Moslems who die in battle in defense of their faith. The Moslem conquests were spread over the world with fire and sword. The Christians, in a certain sense, repaid the Moslems in kind in the Crusades, those strange and, in some respects, glorious phenomena of the Middle Ages. Yet the Crusades in their use of the sword were a complete departure from the Spirit of Christ. It is not without significance that what those mailed knights of the Crusades were fighting for was an empty tomb. The real Christ can never be found with the sword. On one occasion when Jesus had received some discourtesy from a Samaritan village, his two disciples, the two Sons of Thunder, James and John, came to him and said, "Lord, wilt thou that we command fire to come down from heaven, and consume them, even as Elias did?" But Jesus turned and rebuked them and said, "Ye know not what

127

manner of spirit ye are of. For the Son of man is not come to destroy men's lives, but to save them."

There are few hymns that we like to sing better than Toplady's "Rock of Ages" and Charles Wesley's "Jesus, Lover of My Soul." Toplady was a strong Calvinist, and got into a dispute with John Wesley over that great doctrine of God's sovereignty and election. Wesley caricatured Toplady's doctrine in these words, "One and twenty of mankind are elected. Nineteen in twenty are reprobated. The elect shall be saved, do what they will; the reprobate shall be damned, do what they can. Reader, believe this or be damned. Witness my hand, Augustus Toplady." To this unworthy caricature Toplady responded with a pamphlet in which he called Wesley "a perverter of the Truth," and said that under different circumstances a similar forgery would have landed him in Virginia or Maryland.

Of the same sad nature was a dispute between Newman Smith and the great Baptist preacher Robert Hall. In a controversy with Hall on some religious point, Smith wrote a bitter pamphlet, denouncing Hall and his doctrine. Unable to select what he thought was just the appropriate title, he sent the pamphlet to a friend upon whose judgment he relied, and asked him to suggest a suitable title. Some time before, Newman Smith had written a widely read and very helpful pamphlet, "Come to Jesus." When his friend read this bitter tirade against Hall, he sent the pamphlet back to Smith and wrote to him, "The title which I suggest for your pamphlet is this, 'Go to Hell' by the Author of 'Come to Jesus.'" So true followers of Christ and

true friends of Christ, like James and John, forget sometimes the Spirit of Christ.

CHRIST'S PRESENCE WITH HIS CHURCH

This last miracle of Jesus shows his concern for and
his presence with the Church. An earless man would have
been a sad and dreadful spectacle at the Cross. But Christ
prevented that spectacle by touching his ear and healing
him. So he is ever with his Church. Sometimes we wonder
how the Church has survived through the ages—how it has
survived its own blunders and follies, as well as the bitter
opposition and persecution of the world. The secret is that
Christ has kept his promise, "Lo, I am with you always."
He is ever in our midst, making reparation for the wounds,
the wrong impressions, the misrepresentations, which we,
his followers, make to the world. Not a sin is committed
by a Christian, not a bitter word spoken, not a false or
cruel act done, but the hand of Christ is there to make
reparation, and heal our mistakes and misrepresentations
of his Spirit.

SUBMISSION TO THE WILL OF GOD

This final miracle of Jesus not only showed mercy and
forgiveness to a foe, not only protected Peter and the
others of the Twelve from the violence of the mob, not
only saved Christ from misrepresentation, but also showed
on the part of Jesus a beautiful and complete obedience to
the will of God. Just a little before, in his sore agony,
when he had sweat as it were great drops of blood, he had
prayed, "If it be possible, let this cup pass from me:

nevertheless not as I will, but as thou wilt." Now he knew that the cup could not pass. Only by drinking that cup could he make an atonement for the sinner. Therefore, when Peter drew the sword and smote the servant of the high priest, Jesus told him to put his sword into the sheath, saying, "The cup which my Father hath given me, shall I not drink it?"

The sword or the cup? Christ was confronted with this choice. For our eternal good, and our example, too, Jesus chose the cup and not the sword. Still his disciples are confronted at times with this same choice—the sword or the cup? Which shall we take? Shall we take the sword, and claim our right, and defend ourselves, and assail those who do us wrong? Or, following in the footsteps of Jesus, shall we refuse the sword and drink the cup?

CHRISTIAN FORGIVENESS

This last miracle of Jesus was a sublime example of Christian forgiveness of those who do us wrong. Frequently Christ had preached that doctrine, "Love your enemies. . . . Do good to them that hate you, and pray for them which . . . persecute you." Now, at the end of his ministry, he gave a sublime example of how men ought to love their enemies. In some respects it is more wonderful and moving than the prayer he offered on the cross, "Father, forgive them; for they know not what they do." Some of those around the cross hardly understood what they were doing. But this deed of mercy and forgiveness was done to a cowardly foe, the worst kind of foe, the one who strikes a defenseless man. Even Paul, under similar

130

circumstances, when he was on trial before the Sanhedrin, and at the command of the high priest was smitten on the face, could not come up to the measure of Jesus, but answered in indignation, "God shall smite thee, thou whited wall!"

Peter must long have remembered what Jesus said and did there that night in the Garden of Gethsemane; for long afterward he wrote to Christian disciples who were suffering at the hands of their enemies:

If, when ye do well, and suffer for it, ye take it patiently, this is acceptable with God. For even hereunto were ye called: because Christ also suffered for us, leaving us an example, that ye should follow his steps: who did no sin, neither was guile found in his mouth: who, when he was reviled, reviled not again; when he suffered, he threatened not; but committed himself to him that judgeth righteously.

The heaviest burden that one can bear is the burden of an unforgiving spirit. It is a burden, too, which you cannot ask God to help you bear, because it is so contrary to the Spirit of Jesus. There is no greater barrier to the work of the Holy Spirit and the joy of salvation in a man's soul than to harbor the spirit of enmity, ill will, or malice toward any fellow being. Nothing takes you further from Christ than such a spirit. Nothing brings you nearer to Christ than to forgive, even as Christ forgave that man who smote him that night in the Garden of Gethsemane.

During one of the persecutions of the Armenians by the Turks, an Armenian girl and her brother were closely pursued by a bloodthirsty Turkish soldier. He trapped them at the end of a lane and killed the brother before the sister's eyes. The sister managed to escape by leaping over the wall and fleeing into the country. Later she became a nurse. One day a wounded Turkish soldier was brought into her hospital. She recognized him at once as the soldier who had killed her brother and had tried to kill her. His condition was such that the least neglect on the part of the nurse would have cost him his life. But she gave him the most painstaking and constant care. One day, when he was on the road to recovery, he recognized her as the girl whose brother he had slain. He said to her, "Why have you done this for me, who killed your brother?"

She answered, "Because I have a religion which teaches me to forgive my enemies."

I wonder if Malchus, with his healed ear, was in the crowd which stood about the cross the next day when Jesus was dying? Perhaps he was; and perhaps someone standing near him saw with surprise his emotion and said to him, "What do those three fellows, those three malefactors on the cross, mean to you, anyway?"

Malchus may have answered, "I saw that man last night in the Garden of Gethsemane. I was with the mob that seized him; and after Judas had kissed him, I struck him in the face with my fist. Then one of his disciples drew his sword and struck at me. He missed my head, but cut off my ear. And then that man, that one there in the middle, the one crowned with thorns and covered with blood, touched my ear and healed me!"

XI

NATHAN
Preacher to a King

"And the Lord sent Nathan."

II Sam. 12:1

WHEN MAN SENDS HIMSELF, OR SENDS ANOTHER MAN, no startling results are to be expected; but when God sends a man, then great things will happen. "There was a man sent from God, whose name was John." Here is another man sent from God, whose name was Nathan.

Nathan was one of the six chief actors in one of the most moving, most terrible, saddest, most alarming tragedies of the Bible, a book full of stirring, moving, and dramatic events. These are the six chief actors: David, the king; Uriah the Hittite; Bathsheba, his wife; the child born to David and Bathsheba; Joab, David's commander-in-chief; Nathan the prophet. And then there was the supreme Actor himself, God. What a drama this is! Genius, royalty, temptation, sin, conscience, hypocrisy, cruelty, murder; a brokenhearted mother anointing her dying babe with unavailing tears; a father agonizing in prayer; a loyal and heroic soldier treacherously done to death; a great preacher and a great sermon; retribution, repentance, and forgiveness. Where, in or out of the Bible, can it be matched?

That so terrible a chapter appears in the Bible, and in the history of one of the Bible's chief characters, is a proof of the divine origin of the Bible; for what forger or impostor, pretending to write an inspired book, would have inserted such a record of sin and shame concerning David, spoken of elsewhere as a man after God's heart? If this story appears in the Bible, it is because God put it there.

DAVID'S FIRST FALL

A student of literature made it a custom to read through Shakespeare's *Macbeth* once every year, in order that he might warn his soul against the peril that lurks in the pool of imagination and desire, for that tragedy shows how the once loyal and faithful Macbeth became an assassin and murderer. But if one reads the Bible, there is no need of reading Shakespeare or any other literature for warning against sin. Suffice it to say that David was a man of like passions with us. If this happened to the man who wrote the twenty-third psalm, and the ninetieth psalm, then who of us will consider himself above warning?

Some have scoffed at David's being called a man "after God's heart." But this description was written of David long before his fall, and in contrast with Saul; and also long after his fall, in connection with Jeroboam, the son of Nebat, who made Israel to sin. In contrast with either king, David was indeed a man after God's heart, one who desired to do the will of God. How many noble traits he had! He was just, magnanimous, devout; deeply affectionate as a father, weeping alike over the death of the little babe, the child of his sin, and over Absalom, who drove him from his throne and sought to kill him; ever thankful, too, calling upon his soul and all that was within him to bless the Lord and forget not all his benefits. Out of his trials, joys, sorrows, temptations, sins, forgiveness, and restoration, David composed and sang those psalms and songs which, till they shall blend with the angels' songs in heaven, echo all the music of man's soul.

Everybody loved David. If such a man fell into this temptation and sin, his fall locates for us that abyss which yawns ever near to the gates of genius and devotion, as in *Pilgrim's Progress* there was an opening to the pit of hell hard by the gate of the Celestial City.

The natural history and sequence of temptation and sin is clearly stated by James: "Every man is tempted, when he is drawn away of his own lust, and enticed. Then when lust hath conceived, it bringeth forth sin: and sin, when it is finished, bringeth forth death." Lay these verses alongside the chapter of Second Samuel which tells of David's fall, and the consequence of it; and the two passages— James's principle and theory of sin, and David's history in temptation and sin—fit exactly one into the other.

David's fall looks like a sudden fall; but there is always a preparation for such a fall. On an autumn day, going through the woods, you put your foot down upon a fallen log, and immediately it gives way, for the log is rotten. Its collapse is sudden; but months and years of summer rains and winter snows have slowly been corrupting the log and causing it to disintegrate and decay. The Johnstown dam gave way with a roar and crash in a moment of time on that May day in 1889, and two thousand perished in the raging torrent; but for weeks and months the waters imprisoned by the dam had slowly, unobservedly, been eroding the wall of the dam. So it is with moral disasters. There must have been something in David's history before this fall which was preparing the way for it.

The power of temptation depends upon the mood and state of mind in which temptation finds the soul. Jesus said that Satan came to him and found nothing in him. He came to David that fateful evening when David, walking on his roof garden, saw Bathsheba at her bath, and found much in him; the door had been left open. David had seen many beautiful women before this, and under various circumstances; but not with the results of this vision. Hence the necessity of guarding the pool of imagination and desire, and resisting temptation at its first onset. If a spark falls on marble, or ice, nothing happens; it merely goes out. But if the same spark falls on the powder magazine, there is combustion, explosion, and death. So temptation finds the unguarded heart. It was not for nothing that Jesus said, "Watch and pray, that ye enter not into temptation."

As for David's state of heart on the day of his temptation, all we know is that he had passed through his trials and dangers and his long wait and probation for the throne of Israel. He had been crowned king; Saul's house was fallen. God had blessed David with victory and prosperity, and his name and fame were spread abroad in the earth. Perhaps that had something to do with his fall. Prosperity has its perils. After David, one of the greatest kings of Judah was Uzziah, a great organizer, builder, soldier, and administrator. His kingdom reached a degree of power and splendor which it had not known before or after him. Yet the great king Uzziah died an outcast and a leper in the lazar house. And why? This is the record: "But when he was strong, his heart was lifted up to his destruction: for he transgressed against the Lord his God."

When David inquired who the woman was whom he had seen from his balcony, he learned that she was the wife of Uriah the Hittite, one of his soldiers then at the front at the siege of the Ammonite stronghold, Rabbah. Through his valor and courage in battle Uriah had risen to high distinction, for he is named as one of David's thirty-two mighty men. The fact that Bathsheba was the wife of this faithful and courageous officer ought of itself to have given David pause for thought, for the king was the protector of his people, and Uriah was risking his life for his king. But notwithstanding David took the next step into sin, and sent for Bathsheba.

DAVID'S SECOND FALL

What followed the first transgression was far worse than what had gone before. The first sin was one of passion and impulse; but now came two diabolical plots, both hypocritical and shameful. Oriental kings were accustomed to do as they pleased. But David was not just an oriental king; he was the king of Israel. He knew the commandments of God, and knew that he had broken one of them; and he knew also the law of the land. For the sake of his honor and reputation, and perhaps because he feared for his life, David tried to save himself from exposure by making it appear that Uriah was the father of the child who would be born. He sent a command to Joab, leading the army against Rabbah, to send Uriah the Hittite to him at Jerusalem. Joab probably wondered what David wanted of Uriah. Uriah too must have wondered as he left the camp and came to Jerusalem. Perhaps he thought that David had become suspicious of his Hittite origin, for the Hittites were a people accursed to Israel. Or he may have thought that someone had been slandering him to the king. But when he arrived at the palace, he was at once relieved of his fears, for David greeted him kindly, and said to him, "How goes the battle at Rabbah? Are the soldiers of the army in good spirits and in good health?" When Uriah reported how things stood with the army in the campaign against the Ammonites, David said to him, "I am going to give you a brief furlough, for you are one of my most valiant and trusted officers. Would I had more like you! You well deserve a place in my thirty-two mighty men. Go down to your home, visit with your wife, and have a good rest before you return to the front."

Had Uriah got word of what had happened? Was he suspicious of David's motive in sending him down to his house for a rest? No, I think not. But so high was his sense of a soldier's duty that, instead of going down to his house, he slept in the guard room with the king's bodyguard. When David learned this in the morning, he summoned Uriah and inquired of him why he had not availed himself of the royal kindness and rested at his own home, instead of sleeping with the guard. The answer of the noble-minded and loyal Uriah was that when his fellow officers and soldiers were sleeping in the open fields and in the trenches, he did not feel it was proper for him to take his ease at home.

Now David sank still lower. He had failed with Uriah sober; perhaps he could succeed with Uriah drunk. He invited Uriah to spend another day at the palace, and had him eat and drink with him at the king's table. In the long history of strong drink there can be found no stronger indictment of it, and its power to suspend man's reason and rouse his passions, than what we are told here. David plied Uriah with drink until that courageous soldier became drunk. But instead of going to his home when he staggered away from the royal board, he fell down in the guard room and slept again with David's bodyguard.

Now David was desperate. Having failed to foist the paternity of the child upon the husband of the woman, he resolved to slay Uriah, for Uriah dead would not be able to say that the child was not his. In all the known annals of ancient courts, and in all records of wicked kings and nobles, and of murders and assassinations, there can be found nothing worse than the story of the murder of Uriah. The time was short. Uriah must die!

If David had slain Uriah with his own sword, or ordered one of his bodyguards to do so, or commanded Joab to put him to death on some trumped-up charge, that would have been bad enough. But instead of that, David plotted to have Uriah killed in the midst of the battle and fall at the hand of the enemy in the line of duty. To accomplish this, he wrote a letter to Joab. This is the first letter mentioned in Bible history, and the worst in all history. He sent the letter to Joab by the hand of Uriah, who little dreamed that he he was carrying his own death warrant. In the letter David ordered Joab to make an assault upon the Ammonites, and set Uriah in the forefront of the hottest battle; and then Joab and all others in the attacking party were suddenly to withdraw, and leave Uriah alone, so that he would be smitten and die.

Joab carried out this cruel and shameful order. When the trumpets sounded for the attack, Uriah was assigned a place in the van "where valiant men liked to be." At a given signal from Joab, the soldiers fighting by the side of Uriah fell back; but Uriah knew it not, for his eyes were on the foe. On he fought, all alone, smiting down one foe after another, for he was worthy of his place among the thirty-two mighty men. So fighting he fell. Perhaps his last thoughts were for his wife, and for his king. When he died the hero's death on the field of battle, Uriah never dreamed that it was not the sword of an Ammonite that had slain him, but the sword of David his king.

Joab now played his own hypocritical part and pretended to make a formal report to David. The messenger was to tell David of the assault against Rabbah and the repulse of the attacking force. If David showed displeasure, and asked why they came so near to the wall in the battle, and mentioned the fate of Abimelech, Gideon's son, who was slain by a millstone which a woman hurled down on him from the wall when he was attacking Thebez, the messenger was to say to the king that Uriah was among those killed in the battle.

The messenger delivered his message; but, contrary to his expectations, David displayed no displeasure, but in a masterpiece of duplicity told the runner to tell Joab not to be cast down by the repulse and the death of Uriah, "for the sword devoureth one as well as another." I wonder if grim Joab smiled when he received that condolence from David. When Bathsheba heard of the death of her husband, she mourned for him seven days. "When the mourning was past, David sent and fetched her to his house, and she became his wife." "All is well," thought David to himself. "I will give Uriah the burial that a hero deserves. None knows how he came to die, save Joab, and I can count on him not to tell."

Then comes one of the masterpieces of the Bible—the sole comment of the inspired historian on David's dastardly deed; but what a comment it is—"But the thing that David had done displeased the Lord." Forever this brief sentence dismisses the thought that God was indifferent to what David had done. The great historian of the books of Samuel, like Othello, "nothing extenuates, nor aught sets down in malice." All that he does is to relate the facts; and among the facts is this last fact— "The thing that David had done displeased the Lord." Do you ever think of that? that your every deed and every thought either pleases or displeases God?

NATHAN'S SERMON AND DAVID'S
REPENTANCE

Almost a year had passed; but David showed no sign of repentance. We would like to look into David's heart during that year. Sin, once committed, has great blinding and enslaving power. Sin always looks worse in others than in ourselves. No doubt David sought excuses for his heinous sin. Perhaps when that death's-head appeared at the banqueting table, or looked upon him from the foot of the royal couch, David exclaimed, "No; it was not I that slew him. Not I; but the sword of Israel's bitter and accursed foe, the Ammonite. Uriah was not murdered. Uriah died in battle for Israel."

It is impossible to think that a man who had enjoyed such fellowship with God, and such favor from God's hand, could rest at ease after this infamous deed. No; I am sure there were times when David took up his harp to play, but found it so badly out of tune, because his soul was out of tune with God, that he flung it down, and, pacing to and fro on his roof garden, cried aloud, "Would to God that I had never come on this roof that fatal night! Would God that, like Job, I had made a covenant with mine eyes not to think upon a maid!" When all is wrong within a man's heart, the internal distress sometimes will show itself in acts of severity and cruelty. This was so in the case of David. It was after his great sin and before his repentance that David's army under Joab took Rabbah, where Uriah had fallen in battle. Contrary to his usual magnanimity, David treated the inhabitants with great cruelty, torturing them with saws and harrows of iron.

When David went to the front, Joab gave him the heavy crown, studded with precious stones, which the king of the Ammonites had worn on his head, and set it on David's head. But, alas, David, although thou wearest the beautiful crown of the conquered king of Ammon, thou hast discrowned thyself by thy sin!

But whatever David's inner distress and remorse, there was no repentance and no confession. Then the Lord sent Nathan unto David. This was not the first nor the last time that a man of God was sent of God to rebuke a king, and, although his life was at stake, was true to his office. Samuel was sent to rebuke Saul for his folly, and to tell him that God would rend the kingdom from him and give it to David. Moses was sent to rebuke Pharaoh. Elijah was sent with his "thus saith the Lord" to wicked Ahab and bloodthirsty Jezebel. John the Baptist was sent to rebuke Herod Antipas and his paramour, Herodias. Ambrose, the bishop of Milan, was sent to rebuke the emperor Theodosius for his massacre of citizens at Thessalonica, forbidding him to enter the church or receive the sacrament. When Theodosius reminded him that David too was a great sinner, Ambrose answered, "You have imitated David in his sins; now imitate him in his repentance."

Never did a man of God have a more difficult message to deliver. Nathan had been David's friend, minister, and counselor for years. He had encouraged David in his grand project, to build a temple to Jehovah; and then he was sent to tell him that because he had been a man of war, another, his son, should build the temple. As the

143

successor to Samuel, Nathan had seen David increase in power and splendor, and had rejoiced at the favor bestowed upon him by God. But now he must go to him and rebuke him for his sin. I am sure Nathan prayed long and wept much before he preached that sermon to David.

With heavy feet and anxious heart Nathan ascended the steps to the palace, whither he had gone so often before. Had he commenced with a strong denunciation of David for his triple crime of adultery, hypocrisy, and murder, it probably would have aroused the anger of David, instead of working repentance in his heart. But wise Nathan took another course. He knew that David was naturally a just, kind, magnanimous man. Nathan appealed to that sense of right and justice. He appealed to the better man in David. All preachers would do well to study the method of Nathan, and learn how to touch the hidden springs of penitence and remorse.

To accomplish his purpose, Nathan told David the story of two men, one rich, the other poor—so poor that all he had was one little ewe lamb. This little lamb, as the traveler in the Near East today will often see it, was a family pet. It played with the man's children, slept in his bosom at night, and drank out of his own cup. One day there came a traveler to visit the rich man. Instead of taking of his own numerous flock, the rich man, despite the protests of the owner, and the piteous pleas of the children, seized the poor man's lamb and dressed it for his guest.

The parable had the effect upon David that Nathan was sure it would have. It awakened his better nature; it roused his sense of justice. You can see his eye flash

144

and his hand reach for the hilt of his sword, as he exclaimed, "As the Lord liveth, the man that hath done this thing shall surely die; and he shall restore the lamb fourfold!"

So intent had David been upon Nathan's moving tale, that he never thought it could have reference to his own sin. Yet when he said, "The man that hath done this thing shall surely die," David passed sentence upon himself. Then Nathan drove the point of the sword into David's heart—"Thou art the man!"

Now watch David as Nathan showed him why he was "the man." He reminded him how God had delivered him out of the hand of Saul and anointed him king over Israel; how he had strengthened his kingdom and blessed him with power and prosperity. But David had shown his gratitude by a cruel and dastardly crime. "Wherefore hast thou despised the commandment of the Lord, to do evil in his sight? thou hast killed Uriah the Hittite with the sword, and hast taken his wife to be thy wife, and hast slain him with the sword of the children of Ammon. Now therefore the sword shall never depart from thine house; because thou hast despised me, and hast taken the wife of Uriah the Hittite to be thy wife. Behold, I will raise up evil against thee out of thine own house. . . . Thou didst it secretly: but I will do this thing before all Israel, and before the sun."

Never was so tender, but so severe, a sermon ever preached. And what did David do? Had he done as other oriental kings would have done, Nathan's head would have rolled in the dust. But David bowed his head and said to Nathan, "I have sinned against the Lord." But what about Uriah? Yes, he had wronged Uriah; but his sin was against God. As he put it in his penitential psalm, "Against thee, thee only, have I sinned, and done this evil in thy sight." Augustine, asked once how David could say that, when he had so cruelly wronged Uriah, answered, "Because God only is without sin."

When David confessed his sin, the promise of forgiveness was immediate: "The Lord hath put away thy sin." The coming of a soul to true repentance may be a long and slow process; but the forgiveness of God never tarries. David's thirty-second psalm records this immediate forgiveness: "I said, I will confess my transgressions unto the Lord; and thou forgavest the iniquity of my sin." The storm has passed, and the rainbow of mercy spans the heavens. Now angels of heaven, some of whom have not struck a note on your harps since David fell, once again take up your harps, and, sweeping all the chords, sing that sweetest of all songs, the song of the angels rejoicing over one sinner that repenteth!

But Nathan's sermon was not finished. He pronounced full forgiveness for the king; but he also told him that because his sin had made—and still makes—the enemies of God to blaspheme, the sword of temporal calamity would never depart from his house. It never did. In his wrath against the man of Nathan's tale who slaughtered the poor man's lamb, David said, quoting the law of Moses, "He shall restore fourfold." How fourfold was the retribution which fell upon David! See what happened to his four

146

sons: the youngest, the child just born to Bathsheba, who, although he lived so short a time, had wound his little life around his father's heart, was smitten and died; another son, Amnon, who had defiled his sister, Tamar, was slain by Absalom; a third son, Absalom, drove his father from the throne, and then was slain in the battle in the wood of Ephraim, with brokenhearted David, remembering his own transgressions, lamenting over him as he ascended to the chamber over the gate—"O my son Absalom, my son, my son Absalom! would God I had died for thee, O Absalom, my son, my son!" And the fourth son, Adonijah, filled his father's dying chamber with the noise of rebellion, as he tried to seize the throne, and was slain by the fifth son, Solomon.

Yes; David's sin made the enemies of God to blaspheme, and David had to pay. But the sin of David has never made the friends of God to blaspheme. No; it has made the friends of God to sorrow; it has made them be on their guard, not merely against this one kind of sin, but against other sins, and all sins. It has made them say, "If this could happen to the man after God's heart, the man who wrote the twenty-third psalm, and the ninety-first psalm, then what might not happen to me?" It has shown them how sin deceives, blinds, hardens, enslaves. It has made the friends of God say, "Who can understand his errors?" It has made them confess that "the heart is deceitful above all things, and desperately wicked." It has made them say, "Search me, O God, and know my heart: try me, and know my thoughts: and see if there be any wicked way in me, and lead me in the way everlasting."

XII

ONESIMUS

A Fugitive Slave

"For perhaps he therefore departed for
a season, that thou shouldest receive
him for ever."

Philem. 15

SOME YEARS AGO, ON A VISIT TO THE "SEVEN CHURCHES
which are in Asia," I was on my way from Smyrna to
the ruins of Laodicea and Hierapolis. Leaving Izmir, or
Smyrna, and passing on our way the mourning cypress
trees which mark the place where Polycarp suffered
martyrdom, we ascended to the great Anatolian plain and
followed the bed of the Hermus River. On our way,
through the ignorance of our guides, we passed, without
knowing it, the site of Sardis. I had to wait four years
and travel halfway around the world again before I visited
Sardis with its beautifully traced serpentine columns and
its towering citadel.

Turning southward, we came at length to Philadelphia,
which lies up against the Taurus Mountains, which separate the valley of the Hermus River from the valley
of the Lycus River and the Meander River, which, true
to its name, still meanders and winds over the plains until
it meets the sea at Miletus, where Paul delievered his beau-

tiful farewell address to the elders of the church at Ephesus. In the "Letter to the Church in Philadelphia," Christ said, "Him that overcometh will I make a pillar in the temple of my God, and he shall go no more out; and I will write upon him the name of my God." Singularly enough, the most striking and most conspicuous of the ruins at Philadelphia is a tall pillar. Looking upon it, I thought at once of the promise which John had written to the church in Philadelphia.

Leaving Philadelphia, we began the ascent of the mountain range at the foot of which the city lies. Soon the heat of the valley gave way to cool, refreshing, and bracing breezes, and frequently we were in the shade of gigantic pine trees. Near the summit of the mountain I paused to rest for a little and view the grand panorama which opened before me. At the foot of the mountain lay Philadelphia, with its minarets and towers devoted to the worship of the false prophet. Far as the eye could range stretched the valley of the Hermus River. One thought of the empires that had risen and fallen in that great valley.

THE RUNAWAY SLAVE

My mind ran back nineteen hundred years as I looked down the corridors of time. Coming up the same mountain road which I had traversed were two young men clad in Roman garb and full of the vigor of youth. They, too, paused to rest near where I was standing, and turned to look down upon the same far-stretching plains. Each of these young men carried in his garment a letter. These letters would make the name of the city to which they were being carried, and the names of the young men who carried them, and the name of the man who wrote them, immortal. One of these young men was Tychicus, a friend of Paul, who carried Paul's Letter to the Colossians. The other of the young men was Onesimus, who carried the brief, but beautiful, Letter of Paul to Philemon. Today, more than nineteen hundred years after these two young men ascended the mountain on which I was standing, their names are spoken in many churches.

Onesimus is one of the brightest stars in the crown of Paul. Paul had many stars in his crown, and many of them were young men whom he had brought to Christ— Titus, Timothy, Tychicus, Tertius, his amanuensis, Epaphras, Epaphroditus, John Mark, Luke, Aristarchus, Trophimus, Pudens, and others—all young men whom he had introduced to the friendship of Jesus.

None of these attracts us more, or holds greater interest for us, than Onesimus. From Paul's brief Letter to Philemon, and from a reference in the Letter to the Colossians, we learn that Onesimus was a servant, or slave, in the household of Philemon in the city of Colosse. In the Letter to the Colossians, Paul speaks of him as a "faithful and beloved brother." But Onesimus was not always such. Wherever in the New Testament you come upon the word "servant," remember that servant means "slave"; and in an age too when almost every other man in the world was a slave to someone else. Philemon, to whom Paul pays such high tribute as a generous and helpful Christian, must have been a man of some means, for Paul speaks of "the church in thy house," which tells us that the Christian congregation at Colosse used his home as a house of worship. He was noted for his charity, and Paul reminds him that he always makes mention of him in his prayers. A great thing that, to have a place in the prayers of Paul! Yes; and a great thing to have a place in the prayers of any true follower of Christ, however humble he may be.

Onesimus must have held a high post in the household of Philemon. He probably handled the business affairs of his master. But he was unworthy of the trust imposed in him, for he robbed Philemon, and then with his bag of gold fled from Colosse. It was a thousand miles from Colosse to Rome, but Onesimus could not feel that he was safe until he had put those thousand miles between him and the master whom he had robbed. Now he was guilty of two terrible crimes in the sight of Roman law: he had robbed his master, and he had asserted his freedom. He thought that he would lose himself in Rome, that great cesspool of crime and iniquity. But, instead of losing himself in Rome, Onesimus found himself.

At Rome he must have consorted with other criminals and fugitive slaves, always dreading the fate of a slave who robbed his master and fled. He knew well what could be done to him under the Roman law. He could be tortured, crucified, or thrown to the lampreys, as one patrician Roman had thrown a slave who had offended him.

In the providence of God, Onesimus met Paul in Rome. We are not told how this came about. Perhaps he was arrested for some theft or crime he had committed in Rome and was thrown into the same prison as Paul. Perhaps he was recognized on the street by Epaphras, a member of the church of Colosse, who had come with greetings for Paul at Rome. No doubt by this time all his stolen money had disappeared in wild revels in the world's capital. It is likely, too, that Onesimus may have heard Philemon sometimes speak of Paul in his home at Colosse. There is just a posibility, too, that Onesimus himself had seen Paul, and, learning that he was in Rome, counted on his kindness and compassion and sought him out. But however it happened, Onesimus and Paul were brought together. From Paul, Onesimus learned the Way of Life.

Paul speaks of him as a "son whom I have begotten in my bonds." When he came to know Christ, Onesimus was a new man, born again. Hitherto useless and dangerous, now he became a helpful companion of Paul. As many slaves were well educated in that day, ofttimes better than their masters, Onesimus may have read to Paul, or written some of his letters for him. Paul would have liked to keep him as a friend and companion and minister. But when he learned of his past—for Onesimus had told him the whole story—he generously, and with a high sense of honor, sent him back to his master. In view of the seriousness of his crime, Paul sent with Onesimus a letter of intercession and reconciliation on his behalf.

This is the only purely personal letter of the great apostle; and, brief though it is, it throws a bright light on the character of Paul, showing him to be a man of the highest feeling, a gentleman of courtesy and kindness. In the letter Paul prays for Onesimus a kind reception. He asks Philemon to receive him "as myself." For whatever amount Onesimus was indebted to Philemon through his theft, Paul assumes responsibility and gives his I.O.U. to Philemon for the full amount. He asks him to receive him back no longer as a slave, but as "a brother beloved, . . . in the flesh, and in the Lord." He tells Philemon that since he owes his salvation to Paul, he could enjoin him, or command him, but for love's sake he rather entreats him, in the full confidence that Philemon will do more than he has asked. That is a scene I would like to have seen— Onesimus standing before Philemon while the master read the letter from Paul. We doubt not that Philemon did as Paul requested, and that the runaway slave became as useful and helpful to Philemon as he had formerly been useless and dangerous, and that these two, master and slave, were now to one another not master and slave, but brothers in the Lord.

DIVINE GRACE AND THE WORTH
OF ONE SOUL

The electing grace of God in this instance passed over kings and potentates and visited a felon and a slave, for God has said, "I will have mercy on whom I will have mercy, and I will have compassion on whom I will have compassion." How unlikely a convert to Christ was this fugitive slave and thief; as unlikely, one would say, as Paul himself had been; and yet the fugitive slave and felon, and the bitter and prejudiced rabbi who persecuted the Church, both, by the Spirit of God, were brought to Christ. If the hymn had been written then, Onesimus could well have sung it:

153

O Gift of gifts! O grace of faith!
  My God, how can it be
That Thou, who hast discerning love,
  Shouldst give that gift to me?

How many hearts Thou mightst have had
  More innocent than mine,
How many souls more worthy far
  Of that sweet touch of Thine! [1]

In the conversion and salvation of Onesimus we see illustrated in a striking way the value of one soul. Onesimus was only a slave, and a runaway slave at that, and a thief and robber in addition; and yet the great apostle took time out to talk with that slave and show him the Way of Life. Although himself a prisoner at Rome, Paul was, in a way, a world figure. He had the care upon him, he says, of all the churches. He had a magnificent conception of the far-reaching influence and power of the atonement of Christ. "It pleased the Father," he said, "having made peace through the blood of his cross, by him to reconcile all things unto himself; by him, I say, whether they be things in earth, or things in heaven." Yet in that grand conception of the sweep and triumph of the gospel of Christ, Paul did not make the mistake of overlooking the value of a single soul.

We hear much today about "society" and the "nation" and "the world," but these, by themselves and of themselves, are pure abstraction. The one reality is the individual. The tendency of religion in our day has been to

[1] Frederick William Faber.

154

center upon the world, upon human society, and to overlook the significance of the individual soul. Paul did not make this mistake. For a time all his interest was concentrated in the welfare of this fugitive slave. Medieval theology used to say that had only one soul fallen and sinned, still God would have sent his only begotten Son, and the sublime mystery of redemption—the Incarnation, the Atonement, the Resurrection, the Ascension, the outpouring of the Holy Spirit—would have been worked out for the salvation of that one soul. With his own cares and troubles, and his own sufferings, too, Paul had time to talk with this slave and point him to the Saviour. In this respect he was like the Saviour himself, who, dying on the cross and completing the great work of redemption, turned to speak to a dying robber and took him with him into Paradise.

CONVERSION MAKES A MAN USEFUL

When Onesimus found Christ, he became a useful man. Up to that time he had been a useless man and a dangerous man; but now he became a blessing to his fellow man. He became a blessing and a help to Paul, so much so that Paul would fain have kept him in his company. We doubt not, too, that when he returned to his master, Philemon, he became a helpful and useful friend, "in the flesh and in the Lord." Onesimus means "profitable," or "bringing joy." Paul perhaps plays on this name, for he speaks of Onesimus as one who in times past was to Philemon "unprofitable, but now profitable to thee and to me." Rowland Hill, famous Baptist preacher, used to say that he took little stock in a man's piety and religion unless his dog and cat were better off because of his conversion. Onesimus was a young man; and he, like many of those other companions of Paul, shows what Christ can do for a young man. How many thousands of young men there are who, because they have not found Christ, have not found themselves! They are drifting about, ofttimes discontented with what they feel is an imprisoning job or task or calling, with no hope for the future; or they have tried to find excitement and a thrill in the shadowy paths of vice and sin. But when a young man finds Christ and begins to live for Christ, he finds himself and becomes a blessing also to his fellow man.

God said to Abraham of old, "Thou shalt be a blessing." He says this now to every young man or young woman, "Thou shalt be a blessing." When Samuel went to choose Saul for king over Israel, and the humble Saul drew back from that high assignment, and felt himself unworthy of such a noble destiny, Samuel said to him, "On whom is all the desire of Israel? Is it not on thee, and on all thy father's house?" The Spirit of God says this to every young man. "On whom is all the desire of Israel?" There are great things in store for you, a great work to be done by you in life, and a great destiny which awaits you in the life to come. "Thou shalt be a blessing."

THE WORKINGS OF DIVINE PROVIDENCE

In the conversion of Onesimus and his return to Philemon we have a beautiful illustration of the mysterious workings of divine providence, and how God overrules evil for good.

> God moves in a mysterious way
> His wonders to perform.

Paul writes to Philemon, "Perhaps he therefore departed for a season, that thou shouldest receive him for ever." Literally this verse reads: "He was parted from thee for a season, that thou shouldest receive him forever." To Paul there was nothing accidental in the history of Onesimus. He recognized in the whole story the hand of God. In this drama of crime and conversion and reconciliation, as it centered in the fugitive slave, Onesimus, there was another Actor than Philemon and Onesimus and Paul; and that Actor was God.

The crime of Onesimus and his flight to Rome were used of God to bring him to Paul, and Paul brought him to Christ. When he fled that night from Philemon's house at Colosse, taking his master's gold with him, little could Onesimus have thought that the end of this flight to Rome would be his return to Colosse, no longer a slave but a brother beloved, "in the flesh, and in the Lord." Here was one of those acts of providence which men miscall "chance."

The crime and sin of Joseph's brethren, when they sold him for a slave to the Ishmaelites, who took him down into Egypt, and the false and wicked accusation made against him by Potiphar's wife, which resulted in his being cast into prison—all this was used of God in the end, and in

157

a marvelous way, to save, not only Israel, but Egypt too, from starvation. Looking back over it, Joseph said to his brethren, "Ye thought evil against me: but God meant it unto good." In one of his interesting comments on his shipwreck and his stay on the lonely island, Robinson Cruso said, "What a checkerboard of life is Divine Providence."

In the history of Augustine there is a moving example of how God overrules human failure and transgression for the good of the soul and for his own glory. The young Augustine determined to leave Carthage, where his home was, and go to Rome. This was in opposition to the prayers and entreaties of his godly mother, Monica, who prayed so earnestly for his salvation. He deceived his mother by telling her that he was going on board a ship in the harbor to see a friend who was going to sail for Italy. In the morning the ship was gone, and Augustine with it. This departure of her son must have seemed to Monica the refusal to all her prayers. Yet, in the providence of God, it was this visit to Italy which resulted in the conversion of Augustine. Looking back upon it, Augustine said in his *Confessions,* "But thou in thy hidden wisdom didst grant the substance of her desire, yet refused the thing she prayed for [that is, that he might be prevented from going to Italy] in order that thou mightest effect for me what she was ever praying for. She knew not what joy thou wast preparing for her out of my desertion."

Faith in the overruling providence of God throws a bright light on the whole problem of evil. When God created man with freedom of choice and will, he must have foreseen that man would use this freedom to sin. The answer to this deep mystery is our faith in God's providence and his infinite power to bring good out of evil.

PARTED BY DEATH—UNITED IN HEAVEN

I like to take those words of Paul to Philemon, "departed for a season, that thou shouldest receive him for ever," and apply them to the separations of time, when our loved friends are taken from us by death. At first it seems to the bereaved that the separation is final and intolerable. But time and faith do their healing work, and at length the soul comes to rest in the peaceful contemplation of the loved friend who has been taken out of this world into the peace and beauty of the heavenly life. There you can think of them as beyond the "contagion of this world's slow stain," as having "outsoared the shadow of our night." No longer are they subject to change and danger and temptation and suffering. They are "ever with the Lord." Thus, in a real sense, they were parted from you for a season that you might have them *forever*.

I am sure that when Paul said to Philemon that Onesimus was parted from him for a season that he might have him forever, "forever" meant not only the temporary reunion of this life, but also the unbroken reunion of heaven. So let us think of our friends who have been taken from us. They have been parted from us for a season that one day we might meet them in the kingdom of the blessed and be with them forever.

God's providence worked not only in the life of Onesimus; it works in your life and in my life also. Onesimus might have rejected the Spirit of God as it spoke to him when he met Paul in Rome. But, instead of that, he responded to the invitation of the Holy Spirit. He answered the call of God. God's plan for you is wise; his purpose for you is good beyond any power of the human mind to describe. Will you respond to God's purpose for your soul as did that fugitive slave in Rome so long ago?